THE OLD MASTERS

Olivia & Daisy

Printer: CopyTECH(UK) Limited, 15 Culley Ct, Bakewell Rd, Orton Southgate, Peterborough PE2 6XD, UK. Publisher: Elaine Heney, Design Font Apps Ltd, St. Galls House, St. Gall Gardens South, Milltown, Dublin 14, Ireland. www.elaineheneybooks.com This book has been designed and manufactured in accordance with the general safety requirement laid down in Article 5, GPSR. ISBN printed on back cover. EU authorised representative: Elaine Heney. www.elaineheneybooks.com

This Book Belongs to

Books by Elaine Heney

Saddlestone Pony Listening School

Sinead and Strawberry
Roisin and Rhubarb
Conor and Coconut
Fiona and Foxtrot
Quiz book

Blackthorn Stables Junior

Monday, Tuesday, Wednesday, Thursday, Friday, Saturday, Sunday

Blackthorn Stables

January, February, March, April, May, June, July, August, September, October, November, December

The Old Masters

Aisling & Bluebell
James & Jigsaw
Olivia & Daisy
Grace & Chester
Emma & Buttercup
Mia & Mango
Daniel & Dougal

The Connemara Adventure Series

The Forgotten Horse
The Show Horse
The Mayfield Horse
The Stolen Horse
The Adventure Horse
The Lost Horse

The Coral Cove Series

The Riding School Connemara Pony
The Storm and the Connemara Pony
The Surprise Puppy and the Connemara Pony
The Castle Charity Ride and the Connemara Pony
The Shipwreck and the Connemara Pony
The Christmas Connemara Pony

Horse Books for Kids

P is for Pony – ABC Alphabet Book for Kids 2+
Listenology for Kids age 7-14
Horse Care, Riding and Training for kids 6-11
Horse Puzzles, Games & Brain Teasers for kids 7-14
The Galway Connemara

Horse Books for Adults

151 Polework Exercises for Horses
The Galway Connemara
Equine Listenology Guide
Dressage Training for Beginners
The Listenology Guide to Bitless Bridles
Horse Anatomy Colouring Book

Paddy the Pony series

9 Bedtime story books for kids age 0-6

Characters

- Olivia O'Shea, age 12, has a grey Connemara pony called Daisy, age 7.

- Ella, age 12, is her friend. She has a dun Connemara pony called Rose, age 23.

- Finn, age 11 has a grey Connemara pony called Snowy, age 16.

- Ms. O'Leary is the owner of the Killgregory Horse Trekking Centre in Kerry.

- Izzy, age 35. Owns a pink horsebox that has been converted into a mobile library full of horse and pony books. She loves horses, books and history.

- Lucy Mulcahy bought Spotty as an unwanted five year old at a small horse sale in Laois. She is the Irish national eventing champion.

- DJ Declan is the host of a local radio show on Kerry South West Radio.

Glossary

Aids - Signals or cues given by the rider to communicate with the horse.

Collection - A term referring to the horse's ability to shift its weight to its hindquarters for better balance, posture and movement.

Connemara pony - A native Irish pony, originating in the rugged west of Ireland. Legend says Andalusian horses from the 1588 Spanish Armada bred with local ponies. Connemara ponies range from 12.2hh to 15.2hh, but only those 14.2hh or under meet breed standards. Grey is the most common color.

Doublet - A snug, fitted padded jacket made from wool, worn by men from the late 14th to the 17th century.

Dun - A horse coat colour featuring a tan, yellowish, or greyish body with a darker mane and tail, a dorsal stripe along its spine.

Girth - A strap that goes around a horse's belly to secure the saddle.

Grooming - The act of cleaning and caring for a horse's coat, mane, and hooves.

Mounting block - A raised platform used to assist riders in getting onto a horse.

Quadrille - A type of dressage performance involving multiple horses performing coordinated movements.

Self-carriage - The horse's ability to maintain balance and posture by himself, without heavy-handed control from the rider.

Tack - The equipment used for riding, including saddles and bridles.

Trail ride - A ride taken along a designated route, often through natural settings.

Turn on the forehand - A movement where the horse pivots around its front legs.

Turn on the haunches - A movement where the horse pivots around its hind legs.

Withers - The ridge between a horse's shoulder blades, an important point for saddle fit.

Chapter 1

The spring morning air was crisp at Killgregory Trekking Centre in Kerry, as Olivia O'Shea slowly tightened the girth on her grey Connemara pony, Daisy. The familiar scent of hay filled her nostrils as she worked, her long red hair glinting in the early sunlight that streamed through the stable windows.

Daisy turned her head, nudging Olivia's pocket hopefully for treats, her soft muzzle tickling through the fabric of her jodhpurs.

In the stable next door, her best friend Ella was methodically brushing her dun, Rose's coat, until it gleamed in the morning light.

The old mare stood patiently, dozing with one hind leg cocked, while Finn, the other member of their trio, struggled with his pony's saddle pad a few stalls down.

“Argh, why won’t this stay where I put it,” he moaned as the white pad slid sideways on Snowy’s grey back. Finn tried to adjust it again, causing his curly brown hair to fall into his eyes.

"Here, let me help," Olivia offered, giving Daisy a quick pat before walking over.

"You need to centre it more on his withers."

The sound of hooves on concrete outside echoed through the yard as the morning's first trail ride returned from the beach, the riders' happy chatter mixing with the calls of seabirds overhead.

The door to Ms. O'Leary's office across the yard opened, and she emerged, her usually cheerful face creased with worry. She held her phone in one hand and a stack of papers in the other, the morning breeze ruffling the edges as she crossed the yard, nodding at the returning riders.

Her footsteps were heavy as she approached the children, and something about her expression made Olivia's stomach twist with concern.

"Kids, could you come here for a moment?" she called, her voice strained despite her attempt to sound casual.

The children glanced at each other, all thoughts of Snowy's wayward pad forgotten. They slowly began to head towards her. She stood by the weathered wooden mounting block, clutching the papers, her eyes flicking from the few riders dismounting to the papers and back.

The three friends exchanged concerned glances as they gathered around their instructor. Olivia instantly wished she'd brought Daisy with her rather than leaving her in her stable. Something about the pony's steady presence was always a great comfort.

They'd noticed fewer visitors lately; the normally bustling trekking yard had been quieter than usual for weeks, but now it worried Olivia.

The empty parking spaces where horse trailers and cars usually stood told their own story as she glanced at them. Even the waiting list for weekend rides, typically months long, had shortened dramatically in recent weeks.

"Is everything alright?" Ella asked, leading her dun pony, Rose, closer to the group. The old mare's ears pricked forward, sensing the tension in the air.

Ms. O'Leary sighed, her shoulders sagging slightly.

"The bridge to Killgregory Castle Lake is still unusable after the big storm," she explained, running a hand through her greying hair.

"The council says repairs could take months. Our bookings..." She paused, her voice catching slightly.

"Well, they're down by more than half. The Killgregory Castle trail was our most popular ride. I'm sorry, kids, this isn't good news."

Olivia's stomach dropped. With its stunning views of the ancient stone fortress and crystal blue lake, which had been featured in a blockbuster Hollywood movie, the Castle Trail had always been the centre's crown jewel.

Without it they would struggle to get enough tourists to keep the trekking centre going, and she knew it.

"But what about the beach rides?" Finn asked hopefully, his brown curls bouncing as he shifted nervously from foot to foot. He looked up at the few people leading ponies to stables.

"Tourists love those too."

"The beach rides alone aren't enough," Ms. O'Leary replied, shuffling through the papers in her hands.

"And with summer still months away..." She trailed off, looking around at the yard she had built up over twenty years.

"If things don't improve soon, we might have to consider selling some of the horses. Maybe even closing the centre altogether."

"No!" The word burst from all three children simultaneously.

"There has to be something we can do," Olivia insisted, her voice trembling slightly.

She couldn't bear the thought of losing Daisy or watching the other horses being sold off to strangers.

The trekking centre was their second home, where they'd learned to ride and made their closest friends.

"I'm sorry, I just don't know what we can do," Ms. O'Leary said, looking at the bills in her hand.

“I was hoping the council would sort the bridge sooner, but, well, they called this morning saying there wasn't a chance."

The late afternoon breeze carried the salty scent of the sea across the yard, mixing with the familiar smells of hay and horses. A seagull called overhead, its cry seeming somehow mournful in the heavy silence that followed Ms. O'Leary's announcement.

"There has to be something we can do," Ella said, her short black hair falling into her eyes as she shook her head adamantly.

"There just has to be. What if we found new trails? Maybe somewhere else that's just as exciting as the castle trail?"

Ms. O'Leary stood in the stable yard, her weathered hands clasped tightly together as she managed a small, trembling smile.

"You're good kids, and I appreciate the suggestions. But without the castle trail, we're losing our unique selling point.

People come here for that magical experience of riding past Killgregory Castle because they loved it in the movie. The beach rides are lovely, but you can get those anywhere along the coast."

Her voice cracked slightly on the last words.

Beside them the ponies shifted restlessly in their halters. Finn's pony Snowy stretched his grey neck toward Rose, Ella's dun mare, seeking comfort in the tense atmosphere.

Olivia watched as a tear rolled down Ms. O'Leary's cheek, catching the morning light before she wiped it away. The woman had built this place from nothing, turning it into one of Kerry's most beloved riding centres. She'd created something special here, starting with just two ponies and a dream. It couldn't end like this.

"Give us some time," Olivia said suddenly, surprising even herself with the determination in her voice. Her red hair whipped around her face in the spring breeze as she stepped forward.

"We'll think of something. We have to."

“Well, we have a few weeks before I run out of savings,” Ms. O’Leary sighed.

“And I’ll keep going as we are until I do, but then...” she sighed.

“I just wanted you to know.

Slowly, she turned away, heading back to her office. The children stood together for a moment, surrounded by the spring breeze, the salty smell of the ocean, and seagulls wheeling overhead, their cries mixing with the gentle nickering of horses.

“Come on,” Finn took a shuddering breath before turning back to the ponies waiting for them.

Olivia reached for the bolt to Daisy’s door and stopped feeling tears prick her eyes. Daisy's warm breath tickled her neck as the grey Connemara pony snuffled at her.

She looked up, watching other ponies in the arena being tacked up for the next beach ride, their coats gleaming in the morning sun. But the yard felt emptier than usual, with too few ponies being tacked up and too few visiting riders. Suddenly, it was stark and clear.

"We can't let this place close," Olivia whispered, more to herself than to her friends. Her throat felt tight with emotion. Daisy nudged her gently, as if in agreement, and Olivia scratched the pony's grey forelock, taking comfort in the familiar silky strands between her fingers.

"This place means too much to all of us."

Finn nodded solemnly as he adjusted Snowy's girth.

"It's not just about us either. Think about all the people who love coming here, and all the ponies who have such a good home here with Ms. O'Leary."

Whatever it took, they would find a way to save Killgregory Trekking Centre. They had to.

Chapter 2

The kitchen was warm and cosy as Olivia pushed her roast chicken dinner around her plate, her appetite diminished by the day's worrying news. The familiar clinking of cutlery and the gentle hum of Kerry South West Radio in the background did little to lift her spirits.

The evening sun streamed through the windows, casting long shadows across the worn wooden table where her parents sat, exchanging concerned glances at their daughter's unusual quietness.

The delicious aroma of her mother's famous roast chicken, usually her favourite meal, couldn't tempt her tonight. Even the crispy potatoes, golden-brown and perfectly seasoned, remained untouched.

"What's going on, love?" her mother asked.

"The trekking centre might have to close," Olivia finally blurted out, her voice catching. She set down her fork with a soft clink.

"Ms. O'Leary told us today. The storm damaged the bridge to Killgregory Castle, and now nobody can book the castle trail rides anymore. So the centre's bookings are down a lot."

Her mother's hand froze midway to her mouth, fork suspended in air.

"Oh no, that's terrible news! That centre means so much to the community." She reached across the table to squeeze Olivia's hand.

"Ms. O'Leary has run the trekking centre for as long as I can remember. I still have photos of myself riding there when I was your age. It's an amazing place, and Ms. O'Leary takes care of all her horses and ponies so well."

"Surely the council can repair the bridge quickly?" her father asked, his forehead creasing with concern.

"It's a major tourist attraction, after all. The castle brings in visitors from all over the world, especially since that big film came out."

Olivia shook her head, her red hair swaying.

"Ms. O'Leary says it could take months. They don't have the budget for emergency repairs. They called her this morning."

She pushed away her plate entirely, her stomach too knotted with worry to eat.

"Without the castle trail, we might have to sell some of the ponies. Even Daisy could..."

She couldn't finish the sentence, her throat tightening at the thought. She couldn't imagine her life without Daisy and the trekking centre.

"Maybe the council will find the money for the bridge repairs sooner than expected," her father suggested, though his tone suggested he didn't really believe it.

Olivia was about to respond when an announcement on the radio caught her attention, making her drop her fork with a clatter.

"And don't forget, folks!" DJ Declan's cheerful voice announced.

"Cork & Kerry's Top Talent Show is coming up next month. This year's grand prize is a whopping €10,000! Could you be Cork & Kerry's next big star? We're looking for singers, dancers, musicians, and any other amazing talents. Applications close in two weeks..."

Olivia sat bolt upright, her green eyes widening as her heart began to race.

"Did you hear that? A €10,000 prize! We could use that to fix the bridge to the castle!" The possibility made her dizzy with excitement.

Her parents exchanged sceptical looks across the kitchen table. The evening sunlight streaming through the window caught the worry lines on her mother's face.

"Sweetheart," her mother began gently, setting down her own fork, "that's a big competition. There will be people from all over Cork competing. And what kind of act would you even..."

"I don't know yet," Olivia interrupted, her mind already racing with possibilities. She pushed back from the table, too excited to sit still.

"But we have to try something. Maybe we could do something with the ponies? A display or a performance or something..." She paced the kitchen floor, her long red hair swinging with each turn.

"We can't just let the centre close!"

Her father leaned back in his chair, studying her thoughtfully.

“Now hold on, I applaud what you're thinking, love, but I'm not sure even 10 thousand would fix the bridge."

Oliva swallowed hard, glancing at her father.

"Then we can use the money to help keep the centre going until it's fixed."

Her mother smiled at her, glancing over at her father.

"It would take a lot of work," he said.

“And you'd need to come up with something really special to stand out in a competition like that."

"I know," Olivia said, determination settling over her like a warm blanket.

"But Daisy and I, and Ella and Finn with their ponies - we could practice every day after school. There has to be something we could do that would wow the judges!"

The kitchen radio continued to play in the background, but Olivia barely heard it now. Her mind was already filled with possibilities, with dreams of saving the place that meant so much to her.

Tomorrow, she would tell Ella and Finn. Together, they would figure something out. They had to.

****

When she arrived at the yard the following day, Oliva could barely contain herself as she rushed to find Ella and Finn. She had barely slept the night before, her mind a whirlwind of ideas for the show. She heard her friends' voices drifting from the tack room and raced in their direction, bursting through the door to see them sorting through bridles that needed cleaning.

"I've got it!" she exclaimed, her eyes dancing.

"I know how we can save the centre!"

Ella looked up from a dusty bridle, raising an eyebrow.

"What do you mean?"

Breathlessly, Olivia explained about the talent show and the prize money. As she spoke, she could see the doubt creeping into her friends' faces.

"A talent show?" Finn asked sceptically, running a hand through his curly hair.

"But what would we even do? The ponies are great for trekking, but they're not exactly show horses."

"Maybe not," Olivia admitted, "but they're clever, and we know them so well. There must be something we could do that would show people how special they are. This is our chance!"

She glanced through the tack room window, and Finn and Ella followed her gaze. They could see Daisy, Rose, and Snowy grazing peacefully in the spring sunshine, their coats gleaming.

"Think about it," Olivia pressed on, her voice growing more animated.

"We've got three weeks to come up with something amazing. Something that would show everyone just how incredible these ponies are."

Ella bit her lip thoughtfully.

"It would need to be really spectacular to win that kind of competition. We'd be up against singers, dancers, all sorts of acts..."

"I know," Olivia replied, determination glinting in her eyes.

"But we have to try. For Ms. O'Leary, for the centre, for all the ponies." She paused, looking out at their beloved mounts.

"We just need to think creatively. There has to be a way."

“I suppose,” Finn bit his lip.

“If nothing else, it's great advertising. People could see us, the ponies, come for a ride."

“More bookings is more money for the centre," Ella nodded.

“And more money in means Ms. O’Leary can stay open longer,” Finn added.

Chapter 3

The low rumble of an engine drew everyone's attention to the yard entrance, and momentarily, all talk of the talent show stopped. An unusual sight appeared through the gateway - a bright pink horsebox carefully manoeuvring between the parked cars.

Unlike the typical aluminium horse trailers that came to the yard, this one was decorated with painted horses and books along its sides, with "Pony Books Library" written in sweeping, colourful letters.

"What in the world?" Finn whispered, his eyes wide as the horsebox came to a stop.

The driver's door swung open and out stepped a woman with bouncing blonde curls, riding boots, and a bright smile that matched her vehicle's cheerful appearance. Even the ponies in the nearby paddock lifted their heads with interest at the newcomer. Intrigued, the friends slipped out of the tack room and wandered across to the horsebox.

"Hello! I'm Izzy," she announced brightly, waving.

"I run the mobile pony book library. Sorry, I'm a bit late. I had to navigate some very narrow Kerry roads to get here!"

"I'm Olivia." Olivia tucked a strand of red hair behind her ear and reached out a hand, shaking Izzy's.

"I'm Ella," Ella smiled, stepping forward.

"And I'm Finn," he gave a little wave.

“You all have ponies here?” Izzy asked as she fiddled with the metal bolts on the horsebox ramp.

Oliva nodded, pointing to Daisy, who had drifted towards the fence along with the other ponies, keen to see what was going on.

“That’s Daisy,” she smiled.

“She’s a full Connemara.”

"I ride Rose," Ella added, pointing to the older mare.

“She's been at the trekking centre longer than any of us."

"That's my pony Snowy over there." Finn pointed to where his grey pony was watching them curiously from the paddock fence.

"Well, they all look very interested in the box," Izzy smiled, lowering her voice.

“Do you think they'd be interested in borrowing any books?" The children giggled.

Ms. O'Leary hurried across the yard, and then her face lit up with recognition, the first genuine smile they'd seen from her in days.

"Izzy! I got your email last week. I'm so happy you found us. What a wonderful idea this is." She stared at the horsebox.

Olivia, Ella, and Finn exchanged curious glances. Ms O’Leary helped Izzy pull open the pink horsebox's back doors, revealing shelves lined with horse books of all shapes and sizes. The scent of old paper and leather bindings mixed with the familiar stable yard smells of hay and horses.

Daisy stretched her grey neck over the paddock fence, nickering softly at the new arrival, while Rose and Snowy crowded behind her, equally curious about this unusual addition to their yard.

"You're so good to offer this free pony library service to the kids," Ms. O'Leary said warmly, watching as Izzy's blonde curls bounce as she readied the shelves for visitors.

"Actually, the Irish government gives me a grant to run this service," Izzy explained, enthusiastically.

"They love the idea of combining reading with horsemanship. I honestly think I have one of the best jobs in the world - getting to share my two greatest loves: horses and books! Well, kids, would you like to see what books I have?"

The children followed as Izzy led them into the converted horsebox. Warm lighting illuminated rows of carefully organized books. Some looked brand new, while others were ancient, their spines cracked and worn with age.

“Wow,” Olivia eyed the old books. “These look so old.”

"These may be older books," Izzy said, running her fingers along a shelf of leather-bound volumes, "but they are full of wisdom that's just as valuable today as it was hundreds of years ago. The old masters understood that kindness and patience were the keys to working with horses."

She pulled out a particularly old book, handling it with reverence.

"This one's by François Robichon de la Guérinière. He was one of the most influential writers on the art of dressage. He was quite revolutionary for his time!”

Olivia found herself drawn to the old leather-bound books, especially as Izzy began explaining how the old masters had developed their methods through careful observation and understanding of horses' natural behaviours.

"We'll help you bring the books into the tack room, there is a small bookcase in there," Ella offered, already reaching for a stack of books.

As they helped Izzy arrange the books on the tack room shelf, she shared stories of her travels around Ireland, her curly blonde hair bouncing with enthusiasm as she spoke.

"Last week, I was at a yard in Galway where a young girl discovered an old training manual that helped her understand why her pony was struggling with collection. Sometimes the old masters had the best solutions!"

The shelves slowly filled with an eclectic mix of books - everything from modern pony adventures to leather-bound volumes with gold-lettered spines. Olivia carefully handled a particularly old book, its pages yellowed with age.

"That's also one of my favourites," Izzy said, noticing Olivia's interest.

"It's a translation of Antoine de Pluvinel's work. He was one of the first horsemen to write about treating horses with kindness and understanding instead of force. He trained kings, you know!"

Ella picked up a colourful modern novel while Finn browsed through a book about liberty training. The afternoon sun streamed through the tack room window, making the dust motes dance around them as they explored their literary treasures.

"The wonderful thing about horses," Izzy continued, adjusting her collection with care, "is that while our equipment and methods might change over the centuries, the basic truths about working with them remain the same. It's always about patience, understanding, and building trust."

Olivia smiled at her.

"Remember kids," she added as she prepared to leave, gathering her clipboard and signing sheet, "sometimes the best inspiration comes from unexpected places. These books aren't just about riding - they're about understanding, patience, and the special connection between humans and horses. Who knows? Maybe you'll find exactly what you need to understand your ponies better in these pages!"

They followed her out to the yard where the pink horsebox waited, its sides gleaming in the sun. As they waved goodbye, Olivia's mind raced with possibilities.

She looked back at the newly filled bookshelf through the open tack room door, an idea beginning to take shape in her mind. Perhaps somewhere in these pages lay the key to creating something truly special for the talent show - something that would combine the wisdom of the past with their own special bond with their ponies.

"I think," she said slowly to Ella and Finn, "we should start reading. We might find something useful for our act for Cork & Kerry's Top Talent Show."

Chapter 4

That evening, Olivia sat cross-legged on her bed, the old leather-bound book from Izzy's mobile library resting in her lap. The golden letters on its worn spine spelled out "The Maneige Royal" by Antoine de Pluvinel. She carefully opened it, the pages crackling slightly with age.

"This looks so old," she murmured to herself, flipping through the yellowed pages filled with intricate drawings of horses and riders.

The formal language and advanced manoeuvres seemed worlds away from the trail rides she was used to at Killgregory, but something about them drew her in, begging her to read them. She started into the book, but after reading a few pages about proper posture and complex movements she'd never heard of, she set it aside with a sigh.

"Maybe I should look at something more modern," she thought, thinking about all the acts on the talent show and how sparkly and new they seemed. She bit her lip, glancing back at the book. It seemed to call to her to make her pick it up and read it again.

****

The next morning was misty and cool. With Ella at a dentist appointment and Finn helping his dad repair fences, Olivia decided to take Daisy for a solo ride along Killgregory beach. The grey Connemara pony stepped carefully onto the sand as they made their way along the shoreline, the Atlantic waves creating a gentle rhythm beside them.

As they walked along, Olivia's mind drifted to the thoughts of the talent show, the stables, and, strangely, to the old book she'd leafed through the evening before. She barely noticed at first that the mist began to thicken unusually quickly. It wasn't until she could barely see the waves she realized how dense the strange fog had become. She felt her heart quicken a little. An odd sensation washed over her, almost like the world tilted sideways. The sound of the waves faded away; she felt like she was sliding somewhere, but she could still feel the solid saddle and Daisy beneath her.

She closed her eyes, longing for the strange sensation to go away. It did, and slowly she opened her eyes. The mist cleared, and Olivia gasped. She was no longer on the beach - instead, she found herself in an ornate indoor arena with soaring ceilings and highly decorated pillars.

Elegant tapestries adorned the walls, and large windows let in streams of sunlight. Well-dressed men in unusual historical clothing rode beautifully trained horses in complex patterns across the arena.

"Bonjour, es-tu prêt pour ta leçon?" a voice called out.

Olivia turned in her saddle to see a distinguished-looking man approaching her. He was dressed in a red snug fitted padded doublet, dark breeches, and long black leather riding boots.

"I'm sorry, I don't understand..." Olivia stammered her heart racing.

Where was she? What had happened to the beach? “Where are we? What’s going on?”

The man smiled kindly.

"Ah, you speak English. Very good. I am Monsieur Antoine de Pluvinel. Welcome to my Academie d'Equitation in Paris. The year is 1602. Are you ready for your lesson?"

Olivia's jaw dropped as she realized she was somehow in the presence of the very horseman whose book she'd been reading just the night before. She looked down at Daisy, who seemed remarkably calm about their sudden transportation through time.

“Lesson?”

“Oui.”

"But... how? I was just on Killgregory beach a moment ago," Olivia stammered, looking around the magnificent arena in disbelief. Daisy stood calmly beneath her, as if traveling through time and space was an everyday occurrence for her.

Pluvinel's eyes twinkled with amusement.

"Sometimes the most valuable lessons come to us in unexpected ways. Now that you are here, perhaps you would tell me what brings such worry to your young face? I sense you have much on your mind."

Something about his gentle manner made Olivia feel safe despite the strangeness of the situation. She found herself explaining about the trekking centre's troubles, the upcoming talent show in Cork, and their desperate need to create something special enough to win the prize money.

"Ah," Pluvinel nodded thoughtfully, "and you doubt whether your trail ponies could perform anything impressive enough to win such a competition?"

"Well... yes," Olivia admitted, watching a rider nearby execute a perfect pirouette on a magnificent grey stallion.

"We aren't sure what talent we can show." She glanced down at Daisy.

“It needs to be something special,” she glanced at the parading horses.

“Something like what they are doing, but I've never even had a proper dressage lesson. We just do trail rides."

"Mon enfant," Pluvinel said kindly, stepping closer to examine Daisy.

"Dressage is simply about educating the horse to be a willing and harmonious partner. In fact, the word dressage just means 'to train' in French.

Every horse, from the king's finest stallion to the humblest pony, has the capacity to learn and perform with grace. What matters most is the trust between horse and rider. Any display that does such a thing is special, no?" Olivia smiled and nodded.

Pluvinel walked around Daisy, his keen eyes taking in every detail of her conformation.

"When you ride, you must always look straight ahead, above your horse's ears. Your aids, your hands, legs, and seat, should be so subtle that anyone watching would think the horse is dancing of their own accord, performing in perfect harmony with you."

Pluvinel's voice grew passionate as he continued.

"A good rider must develop a feeling of unity with their mount. That special connection that allows you to understand your horse's every movement, every thought. But equally important is your desire to learn, to always improve yourself for the sake of your horse."

He reached out to pat Daisy's neck gently.

"Above all, remember this: patience and gentleness are the keys to reaching the mind of your horse. Be generous with your praise, every time your horse tries to understand you, every time they offer even the smallest correct response, reward them immediately. This praise helps them understand what we're asking and builds their confidence."

A warm smile crossed his face as he watched Daisy lean into his touch.

"You see? Even now, your pony is showing willingness to learn. When we acknowledge their efforts with kindness, they become eager to please, and that is when true partnership begins."

He gestured for Olivia to halt Daisy between two wooden pillars that she hadn't noticed before.

"First, let us work on your position. A correct seat is the foundation of all good riding. Sit as though you were standing on the ground - straight and tall, but without tension."

Olivia tried to follow his instructions, feeling the difference as she adjusted her posture. Daisy seemed to respond immediately, lifting her head and subtly changing her balance.

"Très bien!" Pluvinel praised.

"Now, let us begin with something simple but elegant. You and your friends could create a beautiful quadrille, but we can adapt it to a dance for three horses moving in harmony. Each movement need not be difficult, but when performed with precision and grace, it will be magnifique!"

For the next hour, Pluvinel guided Olivia through exercises that made her feel like she and Daisy were dancing together. He showed her how to ask Daisy to perform a turn on the forehand, where the pony's front legs stayed nearly in place while her hindquarters walked in a circle around them, like the hands of a clock.

"You see," he said as he drew the turn in the school's sand with a stick for her. "She moves around her front feet, staying in one place."

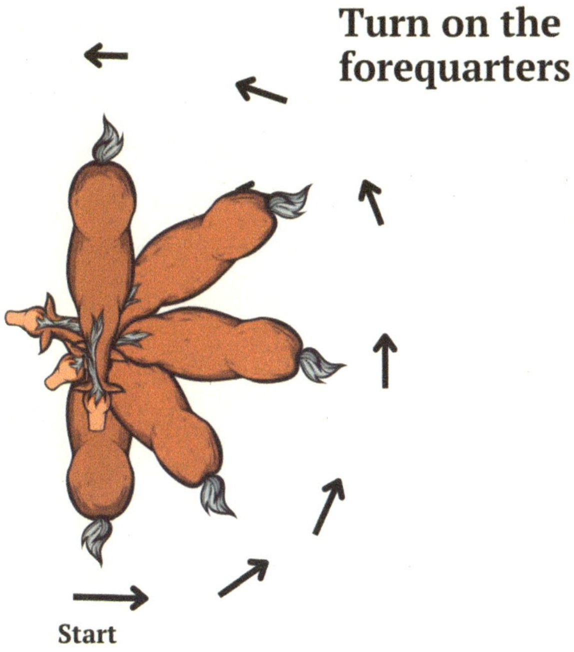

Then they practiced turns on the haunches, where Daisy's hind legs remained still while her front end stepped gracefully around in a half circle.

"The secret," Pluvinel explained patiently, "is to use the lightest possible aids, and to only ask for one step at a time. When asking for the turn on the forehand, ask your horse to look a little to the left, just so you can see the side of her eye, and then a gentle pressure from your left leg just behind the girth asks Daisy to step her hindquarters away from your leg.

At the start, when you feel Daisy even think about changing her balance before she takes a step, you can release and tell her she is wonderful. We don't want to have to use our leg to push her. Instead we want her to understand that a very light touch with our leg is a cue to step her hindquarters to the side.

We want to work with Daisy's mind and make sure she understands our very small cues. Then for the turn on the haunches, you will ask Daisy to rock her weight back a little first, and then if you want to turn her forelegs to the right, you will ask her to look a little to the right with your right rein, still nice and tall, look where you want to go and use your left leg gently to ask her front end to step around, while her right hind pivots in the same place. Like so."

Again, he drew the shapes in the sand for Olivia to see. She smiled and nodded her understanding.

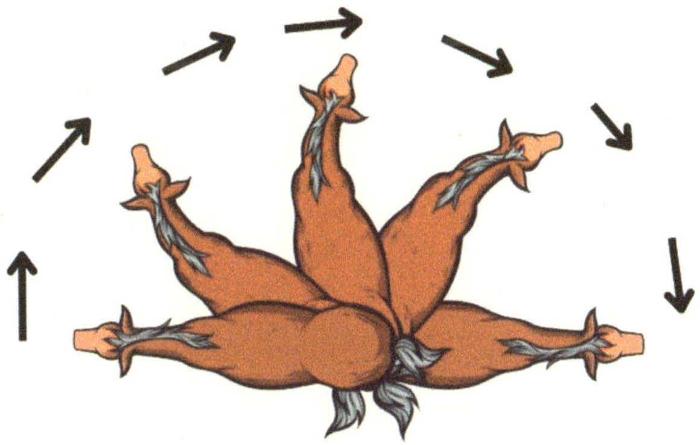

Turn on the hindquarters

As Olivia practiced, she was amazed at how Daisy seemed to understand what was being asked with just the smallest shifts in her position and the lightest touch of her legs. The movements looked far more impressive than they felt. When done correctly, it appeared as though Daisy was pivoting effortlessly on invisible points, creating flowing, dance-like movements.

"Remember," he called out as Olivia and Daisy executed a particularly smooth turn, "be generous with your praise! Every time your pony tries to understand what you ask, reward her effort. Kindness and patience will achieve far more than force or frustration."

Their lesson drew to a close as they managed an almost perfect turn. Olivia smiled and praised Daisy, looking up at Pluvinel with a beaming grin only to see the strange hazy mist filling the arena. The mist began to thicken again, and Olivia felt that strange tilting sensation returning.

"Wait!" she called out to Pluvinel, "I have so much more to learn!"

His voice came through the swirling mist.

"You have all you need to begin. Trust in yourself and your pony. The rest will come with practice..."

Suddenly, Olivia was back on Killgregory beach, the waves lapping at Daisy's hooves. Had it all been a dream? But no, she could still feel the new awareness in her position, and Daisy moved beneath her with a lightness that hadn't been there before.

With growing excitement, she turned Daisy toward home. She couldn't wait to share what she'd learned with Ella and Finn.

Maybe, just maybe, they could create something magical enough to save the trekking centre after all.

Chapter 5

The gravel crunched under Daisy's hooves as Olivia rode back into the yard, her mind still reeling from her extraordinary experience. Her heart was racing with excitement. The morning mist had mostly burned away now, leaving behind a bright spring day that made the puddles in the yard sparkle like mirrors.

Ella and Finn had arrived and were getting the Connemara ponies ready for the next trail ride. Rose stood patiently as Ella brushed her dun coat to a shine, while Finn was checking Snowy's hooves in the corner of the yard.

The familiar sounds of brushes swishing against coats and the occasional stamp of hooves seemed so normal after what had just happened that it almost made Olivia think once again she had imagined everything.

"Hey," Ella called with a wave.

"You'll never believe what just happened!" Olivia called out, sliding down from Daisy's back with unusual grace.

Something about her riding position seemed different, though her friends couldn't quite put their finger on what had changed. Her cheeks were flushed with excitement, and her green eyes sparkled with an almost magical light.

"Where have you been?" Ella asked, pausing with her brush held above Rose's dun coat.

She noticed that both Olivia and Daisy seemed different somehow - calmer, yet more energized at the same time.

"We were wondering if you'd gotten lost in the mist. It came down really thick for a while. We could barely see the beach from here."

Finn looked up from where he was picking out Snowy's hooves, curiosity written across his freckled face.

"Yeah, that was the strangest mist I've ever seen. It almost looked like it was sparkling at one point."

"I had a lesson..." she paused, knowing how incredible it would sound, "with Antoine de Pluvinel."

"Who?" Finn's forehead wrinkled in confusion as he led Snowy over to join them, the pony's hooves making soft crunching sounds in the sand. "Is he local?"

"No! He's a French riding master, from the 1600s!" Olivia burst out, her words tumbling over each other in excitement.

"You know, the one who wrote that old leather book in Izzy's library. The one with the gold letters on the spine?"

Ella and Finn exchanged sceptical glances. “Did you fall off and hit your head?” Finn asked.

Olivia shook her head and took a deep breath, trying to find the words to explain her mysterious experience on the beach, how the mist had rolled in unusually thick, the strange tilting sensation, and her sudden transportation to Pluvinel's magnificent riding academy in Paris. Her voice grew more animated as she described the elegant arena with its soaring ceilings and tapestried walls, the perfectly trained horses, and most importantly, the gentle wisdom of Pluvinel himself.

"He showed me how to ask Daisy to move in ways I never thought possible," she continued, her green eyes bright with enthusiasm.

"And he explained everything so clearly - about using patience and kindness and about rewarding even the smallest try..."

Ella shifted her weight from foot to foot, while Rose nudged her shoulder curiously.

"Olivia," she began carefully, "are you sure you didn't just... I don't know, have a dream last night after you were reading the book?"

"Yeah," Finn added gently, patting Snowy's neck.

"Or maybe you had a daydream while you were riding on the beach?"

"I know it sounds crazy," Olivia admitted, her cheeks flushing slightly. She looked between her two best friends, seeing the concern and doubt in their expressions. "But look - let me show you what he taught me. Then you'll understand!"

She led Daisy to the centre of the yard, making sure she had enough space. With careful concentration, she shifted her position the way Pluvinel had shown her, sitting taller but relaxed.

Almost immediately, Daisy lifted her head, transferred a little weight from her forequarters to her hindquarters and stepped more gracefully with self-carriage.

"And watch this," she said, and with the lightest aids, asked Daisy to perform a turn on the forehand. The grey pony pivoted smoothly, her hindquarters sweeping around while her front feet marked time in place. Then they demonstrated a turn on the haunches, Daisy's front end stepping gracefully around her pivoting on her hind legs.

Ella's scepticism melted into amazement.

"That's beautiful! I've never seen Daisy move like that before."

"And you learned this from a ghost?" Finn asked, but his tone was more curious than doubtful now.

"Not a ghost. It was more like... traveling through time," Olivia tried to explain.

"But that's not the important part. I know how we can win Cork & Kerry's Top Talent Show!" Finn raised an eyebrow.

“We can use what I learned from Pluvinel to create a choreographed routine with all three ponies, like a dance. We can combine these movements with some patterns and transitions. If we make it flow smoothly enough, it will look really impressive!"

"But we're just trail riders on trail riding ponies," Finn protested weakly, though he was already patting Snowy's neck thoughtfully.

"That's exactly what I said to Monsieur de Pluvinel," Olivia replied excitedly.

"But he said every horse and pony in the world can learn to move gracefully - it's all about building trust and using subtle aids. We just need to practice!"

"We could try it," Ella said, staring at Daisy.

****

Over the next week, they stayed late after the trail rides each evening, working together in the yard. Olivia shared everything she remembered from her lesson, helping her friends adjust their positions and teaching them the new movements. The ponies seemed to enjoy the challenge, their ears pricking forward attentively as they learned the new exercises.

"Remember what Pluvinel said about praise," Olivia called out as Ella attempted a turn on the forehand with Rose.

"Every time they try to understand what we're asking, we should reward them!"

Gradually, they developed a routine. They would ride in a triangle formation, then break apart to mirror each other at a distance, incorporating their new movements at specific points. When everything went right, it looked like a carefully choreographed dance.

"It's starting to come together," Ella said one evening, as they cooled off their ponies after practice.

"But do you really think it will be good enough to win?"

Olivia thought about Pluvinel's words about patience and trust.

"We've got three weeks until the show," she said confidently.

"If we keep practicing, and if we really focus on making everything smooth and elegant like he taught me... I think we might have a chance."

“We could add music,” Finn suggested.

“Make it a little more of a show, you know.”

Olivia nodded. As they put their ponies away that evening, the sunset painting the sky in shades of pink and gold, Olivia couldn't help feeling hopeful. She knew that her experience with Pluvinel had been real and the lessons he'd taught her were already transforming their riding. Maybe, just maybe, it would be enough to save the trekking centre.

Chapter 6

A few days later, Olivia, Ella, and Finn were practicing their routine in the grass paddock beside Killgregory beach. The soft spring breeze carried the salt smell from the nearby Atlantic ocean, mixing with the sweet scent of fresh grass. Their ponies' hooves made gentle thuds against the ground as they moved in perfect synchronization.

Ms. O'Leary stood by the fence, her arms crossed and her expression curious. She had come to check on them after hearing about their extra practice sessions, wondering what her young riders were up to.

The evening sun cast long shadows across the paddock as she watched the three friends guide their ponies through movements she'd never seen them perform before.

The three ponies moved with newfound grace and balance. Daisy, Rose, and Snowy executed their turns with fluid precision, transitioning smoothly between movements while maintaining perfect spacing. What struck her most was how light and willing the ponies seemed. Their ears pricked forward attentively, responding to aids so subtle they were nearly invisible.

As they performed a particularly elegant sequence, moving from a triangle formation into mirrored turns on the forehand, Ms. O'Leary's eyebrows rose in surprise. She couldn't help but give a small clap of approval.

These weren't the usual trail rides she was accustomed to seeing. Instead, the ponies seemed to float across the ground, their movements coordinated and purposeful, like dancers in perfect harmony.

Olivia, Ella and Finn sat tall but relaxed in their saddles, as they guided their mounts through the intricate patterns. There was something different about their riding, a newfound awareness and connection with their ponies that hadn't been there before. Even the typically fidgety Snowy was moving with careful precision under Finn's gentle guidance.

"Hold on a moment," Ms. O'Leary called out, waving them over from where she stood by the paddock fence.

The three friends exchanged nervous glances before guiding their ponies toward her. The sun cast long shadows across the sand, and a gentle breeze carried the salty scent of the ocean.

"Where did you learn to ride like that?" she asked, her eyes wide with wonder. She leaned forward against the wooden rail, studying their movements intently.

"I've been teaching riding for twenty years, and I've never seen our trail ponies move with such balance and self-carriage. And your positions - you're all sitting so differently! The way those ponies are carrying themselves... it's like they're floating!"

Olivia felt her cheeks flush with pride as she gave Daisy a gentle pat on her grey neck. She could feel how differently the pony moved beneath her now, so much lighter and more responsive to the smallest aids.

Beside her, Rose and Snowy stood quietly but alertly, their ears pricked forward with interest.

"We've been studying some old dressage books from Izzy's mobile library," she explained carefully, exchanging a quick glance with Ella and Finn.

She decided it was best to omit her mysterious encounter with Pluvinel. That would be hard to explain, especially to a grown-up.

"We wanted to try something different with the ponies."

“Well, I’d say you achieved it,” Ms. O’Leary smiled. “They looked wonderful.”

Olivia blushed. She took a deep breath.

"Actually, we're preparing something for Cork & Kerry's Top Talent Show. We thought... well if we could win the prize money, it could help pay to get the bridge fixed. Or at least keep the centre going until it is fixed."

Ms. O’Leary smiled, her eyes going a little misty. Olivia's voice grew stronger as she went on.

"The first prize is ten thousand euros."

Ms. O'Leary's eyebrows rose in surprise as she looked between the three young riders and their attentive ponies. The determination on their faces touched her heart - these children were working so hard to help save the place they loved.

She noticed how Ella sat forward eagerly in her saddle while Finn nodded along, both clearly invested in their friend's plan. Even the ponies seemed to sense the importance of the moment, standing quietly but alertly, their ears pricked forward.

The familiar sounds of waves breaking on the beach provided a gentle backdrop to her words, reminding them all of exactly what they were fighting to preserve, this magical place where children and ponies could experience the joy of riding along the beautiful Kerry coastline.

"You know," Ms. O'Leary smiled, "I've watched a lot of high-level dressage competitions over the years," she said thoughtfully, running her hand along the weathered fence rail.

"And I often come away feeling disappointed. So many riders use force to achieve their movements, harsh bits, tight nosebands, spurs." She shook her head sadly.

"But you three..." she gestured at them with admiration, her eyes bright with emotion.

"You've got your ponies dancing with just the lightest touch. Look at how their ears are forward, how relaxed their expressions are. They're happy and willing partners in this - to me that's real horsemanship."

"Really?" Finn asked, his face breaking into a grin as he patted Snowy's neck. The grey pony turned his head to sniff his hand affectionately.

"Really," Ms. O'Leary confirmed, watching how Rose shifted her weight to stay close to Ella, and how Daisy's ears flicked back to catch Olivia's quiet voice.

"Some of those top dressage riders could learn a thing or two from watching how you've taught these movements while keeping your ponies so soft and responsive. There's no tension, no resistance - just harmony between horse and rider. That's what all horse riding is supposed to be."

“So, do you think we stand a chance?” Ella asked.

Ms. O’Leary smiled. “As good a chance as anyone.”

The three friends sat a little taller in their saddles, exchanging proud glances. Their ponies seemed to sense their riders' joy, lifting their heads with confidence.

"OK. Show me your routine from the beginning," Ms. O'Leary said, stepping back from the fence to get a better view. Her eyes sparkled with interest as she added, "I want to see everything - every transition, every movement. Something tells me this could be quite special."

As they moved into their starting position, forming their signature triangle formation, Olivia felt a surge of hope.

Daisy's steps beneath her were light and eager, ready to dance. With Ms. O'Leary's approval and Pluvinel's teachings guiding them, perhaps they really could create something magical enough to save Killgregory trekking centre.

Chapter 7

The rain drummed steadily against the roof of the tack room where Olivia, Ella, and Finn huddled together, watching the water stream down the windows. It had been raining non-stop in Kerry for five days, turning the paddocks into a muddy mess and making it impossible to practice their routine. Outside, their ponies stood in their field shelters, peering out at the puddles growing bigger with every hour.

They had tried to ride out on the beach, but it was miserable and wet. The ponies just wanted to keep their tails tucked, and their hindquarters faced the driving rain. There was no chance to practice for the show.

"At this rate, we'll never be ready for Cork & Kerry's Top Talent Show," Finn sighed, his usual cheerful expression dampened by the weather. Through the window, they could see the rain pouring down.

"We've only got two weeks left," Ella added, absently braiding a piece of baling twine.

"And we still don't have it perfect yet."

The tack room door suddenly burst open, bringing with it a gust of wet air and Ms. O'Leary's excited voice.

"Children! Come quick - there's someone I want you to meet!"

They exchanged glances and then hurried outside, pulling their rain jackets tight around them. A sleek Landy was parked in the yard, and beside it stood a tall woman with short brown hair, wearing smart riding clothes beneath her waterproof coat. Olivia recognized her immediately from magazine covers and news reports.

"Lucy Mulcahy!" she gasped. Finn frowned a little.

“You know, the Irish national eventing champion!”

Finn’s eyes went wide.

“I didn’t recognize her without her riding hat and Spotty.”

Lucy smiled warmly at them, the rain pouring down her coat, and Ms. O'Leary quickly gestured toward her house.

"Let's all get out of this weather and have a proper chat over a cup of tea," she called out over the drumming of raindrops.

"We're all getting soaked out here!"

They hurried across the yard to Ms. O'Leary's cosy cottage, their boots squelching in the puddles and rain dripping from their hair. Inside, the warmth enveloped them like a hug.

The kettle whistled cheerfully on the old stove, and the kitchen was filled with the comforting aroma of freshly baked scones. The rain drummed steadily against the windows, making the cottage feel even more snug and welcoming.

As they took off their wet coats, hanging them on the row of wooden pegs by the door, Ms. O'Leary moved around her kitchen, pulling out some mugs and arranging the scones on pretty floral plates.

The kitchen itself was exactly what you'd expect in an Irish riding school, well-worn but spotlessly clean, with rosettes and photos of horses covering one wall.

Lucy took a seat at the sturdy oak kitchen table, its surface marked with decades of tea cups and conversations. She looked completely at home, despite being a national champion, as she helped herself to a scone and watched the children with genuine interest.

"Ms. O'Leary's been telling me all about your routine," Lucy said, her eyes twinkling warmly as she spread clotted cream on her scone.

"And about the bridge situation. It's quite impressive what you're trying to do." She paused thoughtfully, stirring her tea.

"Thanks," Olivia managed, her voice shaking slightly with nerves.

"So I had an idea that might help. I've got an indoor arena just sitting empty this week. Spotty and I are taking a bit of a break after the championships. The footing's perfect and there's plenty of space. Would you like to use it for your practice? It would be a shame to let all your hard work go to waste because of the rain."

The three friends stared at her in amazement. Everyone knew about Lucy and Spotty's incredible journey. How she'd discovered him at a small horse sale in Laois, unwanted and nervous, and transformed him into a championship eventer through patience and understanding.

"Really?" Ella squeaked, her eyes wide with excitement.

"Of course! In fact..." Lucy's smile widened, "I'd love to watch your routine sometime too!"

****

Over the next few days, Lucy's indoor arena became their sanctuary from the rain. The space was magical - mirrors lined one wall, the footing was perfect, and most importantly, it was dry. Their ponies seemed to float across the surface, their movements becoming more refined with each practice.

"That's it!" Lucy called out one afternoon, watching from the centre of the arena.

"I love what you told me about Pluvinel's teachings - it's all about harmony and understanding. That's my goal with Spotty, too. Keep it up!"

"What seems more dreamlike," Ella asked Olivia as they set up to practice again.

"Being here in Lucy and Spotty's private school or visiting France and Pluvinel?"

Olivia smiled, not entirely sure how to answer her friend's question. Each seemed as unreal as the other.

****

A few days later, Finn met Olivia and Ella at the trekking centre, waving his phone, a worried look on his face. He darted across the field to where Olivia and

Ella were catching the ponies, his curly brown hair brushed back by the wind and his mad dash towards them, his face flushed with concern.

"Have you seen this?" he called out, slightly out of breath.

"The Dublin Irish Dancing Champions have entered Cork & Kerry's Top Talent! Apparently, three of their lead dancers are originally from Cork, so they're allowed to compete under the local talent rules. They're saying it's a 'homecoming performance' or something like that."

They huddled around his phone in the yard, their shoulders touching as they watched the video. The Dublin dance troupe moved across the stage like a perfectly coordinated machine. Twelve dancers in elaborate sparkly costumes that glinted under the stage lights. Their synchronized movements were flawless, feet flying in perfect unison as they performed complicated steps that seemed to defy gravity.

The routine built to a crescendo with the dancers weaving between each other at lightning speed, their timing perfect down to the millisecond. When they launched into their finale - a spectacular series of synchronized leaps and turns that seemed to float in the air - the audience erupted in thunderous applause.

Behind them, their ponies shifted curiously, wondering why their riders were clustered around the small glowing screen instead of bringing them in to get tacked up. Daisy stretched her neck over Olivia's shoulder to investigate, her soft muzzle tickling her rider's ear.

"How can we compete with that?" Ella whispered, her face pale as she unconsciously reached back to pat Rose's dun neck for comfort.

"They're professionals! Look at their costumes, their training... they've probably been practicing for years. We're just three kids with trail ponies who learned some new moves a few weeks ago."

Olivia felt doubt creeping in too, but then she remembered Pluvinel's words about patience and trust. She watched their ponies waiting quietly nearby, Daisy, Rose, and Snowy, who had learned to move with such grace and willingness.

They weren't just performing tricks, they were demonstrating the beautiful partnership between horse and rider that Pluvinel had taught her about.

"Maybe we can't match their technical perfection," she said slowly, "but we have something different. Something special." She patted Daisy's neck, feeling the pony's warm breath on her hand.

"We have the magic of three ponies dancing together in perfect harmony with their riders. When was the last time anyone saw something like that at a talent show?"

Chapter 8

After a week of relentless rain, the sun finally broke through the clouds, casting golden light across the paddock beside Killgregory Beach. It had been quite windy for the last few days, so the ground had mostly dried out, and the paddock was ok to ride in again and practice their routine. Seagulls wheeled overhead, their calls mixing with the distant sound of waves breaking on the shore.

But something wasn't right. While Ella and Finn guided Rose and Snowy through their movements with newfound confidence, Olivia struggled to keep Daisy balanced.

The grey pony kept leaning heavily on the bit, pulling against Olivia's hands and throwing off their carefully practiced timing.

"Let's try it again," Olivia called out, trying to keep the frustration from her voice. But as they moved into their signature triangle formation, Daisy's head dropped down, her weight falling onto the forehand. The pony's previously light, dancing steps had become heavy and unbalanced.

"Maybe we should take a break," Ella suggested kindly, watching her friend's mounting frustration. Rose stood quietly beneath her, ears pricked forward attentively.

"You go ahead," Olivia replied, dismounting to adjust Daisy's girth.

"There's something I need to do."

After her friends had dismounted and led their ponies away, Olivia pulled out the worn copy of Pluvinel's book from her saddle bag. She flipped through the pages desperately, searching for something she might have missed about balance and self-carriage.

But the elegant illustrations and careful instructions that had seemed so clear before now felt confusing and out of reach.

Sighing heavily, she closed the book and swung back into the saddle.

"Come on, girl," she murmured to Daisy, "let's go for a ride on the beach to clear our heads."

They headed down to Killgregory beach, where the tide was out and the wet sand stretched endlessly ahead of them. The late afternoon sun was starting to sink toward the horizon, casting long shadows across the shore.

As Olivia guided Daisy down the path to the beach, she spotted a familiar figure in the distance - Lucy Mulcahy aboard her famous eventer, Spotty, walking up from the waterline. The championship horse's bay coat gleamed in the golden light as they approached.

"Hello Olivia, it's nice to see you again! Is everything OK? I saw Ella and Finn heading back to the yard earlier." Lucy called out, bringing Spotty to a halt beside them.

The big horse's ears pricked forward curiously at Daisy, who lifted her head to return his greeting.

"Oh, yes," Olivia replied, trying to sound convincing.

"I just thought I'd take a ride on the beach to clear my head a bit." She absently stroked Daisy's grey neck, not quite meeting Lucy's eyes.

Lucy studied her for a moment with understanding.

"Sometimes that's exactly what we need - just us and our horses and the open beach. Spotty and I do our best thinking out here." She smiled warmly before gathering her reins.

"Enjoy your ride. The tide is perfect for a nice long canter if you're up for it."

Olivia watched as Lucy and Spotty continued up the beach path, their shadows stretching long behind them. The sound of waves lapping at the shore called to her, and she turned Daisy toward the vast expanse of sand ahead.

"It's just you and me now, girl," Olivia murmured, leaning forward to stroke Daisy's grey neck. The pony's ears flicked back at the sound of her voice.

"I know we're struggling with the routine, but we'll figure it out together. You're trying so hard for me."

The grey pony's ears pricked forward with interest as the mist thickened around them. Daisy shifted her weight slightly, pressing her warm shoulder against Olivia's leg as if offering comfort.

"You're the best pony I could ever ask for," Olivia continued softly, running her fingers through Daisy's silvery mane.

"I love you just the way you are. We're a team, aren't we?"

As if in answer, Daisy let out a gentle snort and turned her head to nudge Olivia's boot affectionately. Olivia felt that strange sensation again - like the world was shifting slightly sideways, the colours becoming both sharper and softer at the same time. Her head felt light and tingly.

As they walked along the water's edge, Olivia noticed a familiar mist beginning to roll in from the sea, curling around Daisy's legs in ethereal wisps.

The mist swirled higher, and Daisy's steady footsteps seemed to echo strangely in the thickening air. Olivia's heart began to race as the familiar dizziness washed over her. What was happening? Surely she wasn't...

Chapter 9

Olivia felt a familiar spinning sensation, and when the world steadied again, she found herself and Daisy in a very different place. She was back in the elegant indoor arena of Pluvinel's Academie d'Equitation in Paris, 1602.

Monsieur de Pluvinel stood in the centre of the sand arena, dressed in his characteristic red doublet, dark breeches with gleaming black leather boots. His kind eyes lit up with recognition as he saw them materialize.

"Ah, my young friend! Welcome back," he called out warmly, walking over to greet them.

"But what is wrong? I can see something troubles you."

Olivia slid down from Daisy's back, her legs slightly shaky from the time travel. The grey pony dropped her head to sniff curiously at the arena footing, which was different from the sand at the beach.

"Monsieur de Pluvinel," Olivia started, her words tumbling out.

"We've been practicing our routine for the talent show, but Daisy keeps leaning on my hands and feeling heavy. And now we've just found out that the Irish National Dance Champions from Dublin are entering the competition! And they're amazing. How can three kids with trekking ponies possibly compete with professional dancers?

If we don't win the prize money, Ms. O'Leary won't be able to rebuild the bridge to access Killgregory Castle. Without those trail rides, the trekking centre can't survive." Her voice cracked slightly as she continued.

"And Ms. O'Leary will have to close down and sell all the ponies. I can't bear the thought of losing Daisy. She's my best friend. Everything depends on us winning this competition, but how can we when we're up against professionals? And Daisy and I are having big problems. It's just not working anymore. "

Pluvinel listened thoughtfully, stroking his neat beard.

"That is a lot. Now, let us first put aside our worries we cannot fix and see about the ones we can. Let us address your pony's balance. Come, bring her here." He gestured toward the arena wall.

"I have an exercise to show you that may help. It is called a volte renversee. It will help your pony learn to shift her weight back onto her hindquarters instead of leaning forward and feeling heavy in your hands," he explained.

"First you will ask Daisy to walk a circle, not too large. Now as she walks in a circle, we would like her two front legs to be on the circle and her two hind legs to be on a slightly larger outer circle.

With this exercise when she moves sideways while maintaining forward motion, she must engage her inside hind leg more deeply under her body. When I say inside leg, I always mean the hind leg on the inside of the bend of the horse's body."

Under his patient guidance, Olivia followed his instructions.

"First walk your pony on a circle to the left. Use your left rein a little to ask Daisy to look a little to the inside of the circle. You should just be able to see the side of her left eye. That's perfect," he smiled.

The grey pony seemed puzzled at first but tried her best to understand.

"Now we want a slight left bend in Daisy's body. To do this, I want you to keep your shoulders level, but have just a tiny bit more weight in your left seat bone. That's it. Daisy's back muscles on the left under your left seat bone will contract a little, causing a little bend to the left in her body. Super."

Pluvinel watched the grey mare closely as Olivia followed his instructions carefully.

"Now I would like you to use only your left leg, and push Daisy's hindquarters a little to the outside of the circle. That's it! Now her two front legs are doing one circle, but her two hind legs are doing a slightly larger circle!"

Olivia pictured Daisy in her mind doing as Pluvinel had instructed.

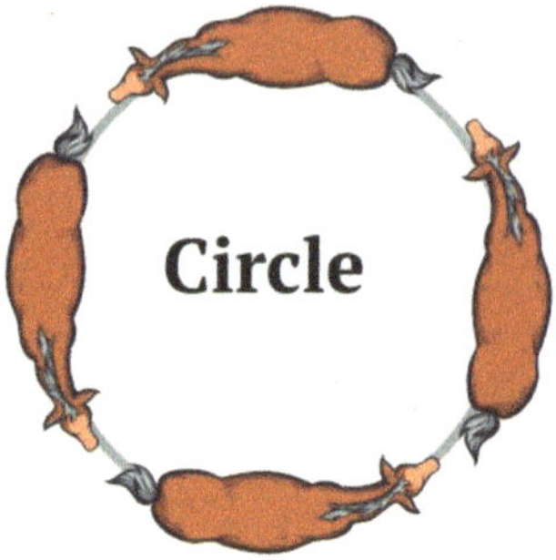

Circle with the hindquarters on a large circle

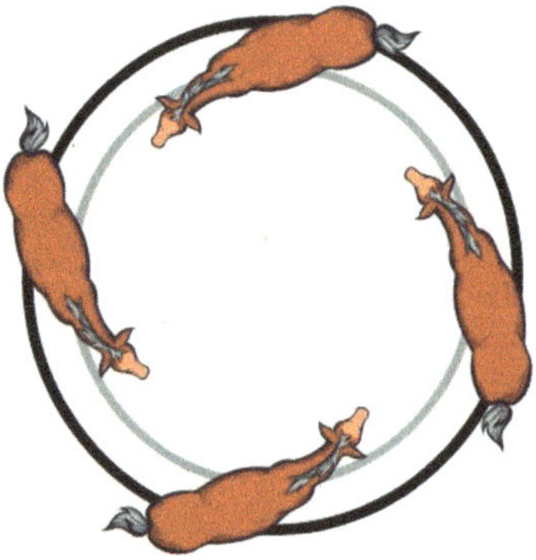

“This exercise is really good as it asks Daisy to step her inside hind leg (her left hind in this case) further under her body than she does normally.

This changes her posture. Now she has to carry a little more weight on her hindquarters, and a little less weight on her forequarters. So with a little practise, she will feel lighter in your hands, and more collected."

"Of course we do it both ways. When she understands doing this with a left bend, then we do a circle to the right, and again ask her hindquarters to move to make a bigger circle track, than her two front legs. So when you are doing a circle like this to the left, the rider uses their left rein, left seat bone and left leg. And when you do a circle like this to the right, the rider uses their right rein, right seat bone and right leg. "

"But Monsieur," Olivia asked, "Daisy's just a trail pon. Does she really need to learn collection?"

Pluvinel's eyes twinkled.

"My dear, every horse and pony benefits from good balance and posture, just as every person does. Whether they carry knights into battle or children along peaceful trails, a well-balanced horse will stay sound and happy for many years."

He demonstrated how to use her leg and rein aids subtly.

"Besides," he added with a smile, "these elegant movements will certainly impress your talent show judges!"

As they practiced, Daisy began to understand what was being asked. Her steps became lighter, and Olivia could feel her starting to carry herself differently.

"Excellent!" Pluvinel praised.

"Now, let me show you something else that will add grace to your performance."

He demonstrated how to gather her reins in her left hand, her thumb holding the reins while her other fingers could touch either rein for more subtle communication.

"Your right hand rests just above your left hand, in the centre of your body, holding the ends of the reins. This creates an elegant picture - as if your pony dances of her own accord, with barely visible guidance from you. It is one thing to do advanced manoeuvres with two hands - but it is much more impressive to do them one handed!"

After more practice, Olivia could feel the difference in Daisy's way of going. The pony seemed proud of herself, carrying her head with new confidence.

"Remember," Pluvinel said as the mist began to gather again, "true grace comes from harmony between horse and rider. Your ponies' willing partnership and happiness with you is far more beautiful than any advanced manoeuvre."

The last thing Olivia saw before the mist enveloped them completely was Pluvinel's encouraging smile and slight bow. Then they were back on Killgregory beach, the setting sun painting the sky in brilliant oranges and pinks.

Daisy shook her head, sending her forelock dancing, and Olivia could have sworn the pony looked rather pleased with herself.

"Come on, girl," she said, gathering her reins in one hand, the way Pluvinel had shown her.

"Let's go show the others what we've learned. They are never going to believe what just happened!"

Chapter 10

The next morning dawned bright and clear as Olivia led Daisy into the paddock where Ella and Finn were already warming up their ponies. Her heart felt lighter than it had in days, buoyed by her secret lesson with Pluvinel.

“We got this,” she whispered to Daisy with a nod.

“Hey,” she waved to her friends. They waved back as she came closer.

"We have something to show you,” she smiled.

“Watch this!" Gathering her reins in her left hand as Pluvinel had taught her, she guided Daisy into a volte renversee. The grey pony moved with newfound grace, her steps light and balanced.

"That's amazing!" Ella exclaimed, bringing Rose to a halt to watch.

"How did you get her going so differently?"

Olivia was about to answer when she spotted Ms. O'Leary hurrying across the yard toward the paddock gate, her wellington boots squelching in the damp grass. Her face was lit up with excitement as she waved enthusiastically to get their attention.

"Kids! Come here - you won't believe this!" Ms. O'Leary called out, slightly out of breath from her quick walk. The three friends exchanged curious glances before guiding their ponies over to where she stood.

"I've just had the most wonderful phone call," Ms. O'Leary continued, her eyes sparkling.

"DJ Declan from Kerry South West Radio wants you all on his morning show tomorrow! He's heard about your entry in the Cork & Kerry's Top Talent Show and wants to interview you about it!"

"Really? On actual radio?" Ella squeaked, her eyes widening.

"The same show my mother listens to every morning while making breakfast?" Finn asked in disbelief.

"The very same," Ms. O'Leary nodded, grinning at their reactions.

"He wants you there at eight o'clock tomorrow morning. It's a great chance to tell everyone about what you're doing and why. Maybe we can even drum up some local support for the trekking centre!"

Olivia felt a mixture of excitement and nervousness flutter in her stomach. They'd be talking live on air to thousands of listeners across Kerry!

"This is brilliant!" she said, her earlier worries momentarily forgotten in the thrill of the news.

"Wait until I tell my parents. They're never going to believe it!"

She reached down to pat Daisy's neck, drawing comfort from the pony's solid presence beneath her.

****

The very next morning, Olivia found herself sitting nervously in the radio station's studio, along with Ella and Finn. They were surrounded by microphones and mysterious equipment with blinking lights. DJ Declan, a friendly man with laugh lines around his eyes, adjusted their microphones and gave them a reassuring wink.

"And we're back with some super special guests today, three young riders from Killgregory Trekking Centre who are taking on quite a challenge!" His voice took on the smooth, professional tone they'd heard so often on the radio.

"So, tell us about this competition you're entering."

Ella spoke first, her voice slightly shaky but growing stronger.

"Well, we're entering Cork & Kerry's Top Talent Show with our ponies. We've created a special routine that combines riding skills with music."

"But this isn't just for fun, is it kids?" DJ Declan prompted.

"There's quite a lot riding on this competition if you'll pardon the pun!"

Finn leaned toward his microphone.

"The prize money would help save our trekking centre. We need to rebuild an old bridge to access the Killgregory Castle trail again. Or at least keep the centre going until the council can get it fixed."

The interview continued in the cosy radio studio, with DJ Declan leaning forward in his chair, genuinely interested in their story. His warm, friendly voice put them at ease as he asked questions about their ponies and their preparation for the competition.

"So tell us about your ponies," DJ Declan encouraged, adjusting his headphones.

"What makes them special?"

Olivia spoke first, her voice growing confident as she talked about her beloved grey pony.

"Daisy is a Connemara pony. She might look like an ordinary trekking pony, but she's amazing. She tries so hard to learn new things, and she's got the kindest heart."

"And Rose is the sweetest Connemara pony ever," Ella chimed in, her eyes sparkling.

"She's older, but she still loves learning new things."

Finn nodded enthusiastically.

"Snowy's the same. He's a Connemara too. He is really clever and picks up the moves so quickly!"

DJ Declan smiled warmly.

"It sounds like you've got quite the special team of Connemara ponies there. And you're all working hard to save Killgregory Trekking Centre?"

"Yes," Olivia explained, her voice passionate.

"Without the bridge to access the Killgregory Castle trail, the centre isn't getting the number of visitors it usually does and might have to close. These ponies are our best friends, so we just can't let that happen."

By the time they left the studio, walking out into the bright morning sunshine, they were floating on air.

The excitement of being on live radio, sharing their story with all of Kerry, had left them buzzing with energy and hope. Maybe, just maybe, their dream of saving the trekking centre wasn't so impossible after all.

"I can't believe we were just on Kerry radio!" Ella exclaimed, practically skipping down the street.

"Did you hear how many people called in to wish us luck?" Finn added, grinning from ear to ear.

Olivia couldn't stop smiling. The support from their local community felt like a warm hug, giving them renewed determination to face the challenge ahead.

****

A few days later, Olivia, Ella and Finn gathered in the tack room after their morning ride. Finn noticed the local newspaper sitting on the bench and grabbed it excitedly.

"Look! We made the front page!" he exclaimed, holding up the Kerry Chronicle. There they were, sitting proudly on their ponies on Killgregory beach, the castle visible in the misty background.

But as they read the article, their excitement faded. The reporter had written:

"While these plucky young riders show admirable spirit, one has to question their chances against the current Irish National Dance Champions. Can three ordinary trekking ponies from Kerry really compete against professional Irish dancers who have won multiple international awards? The Dublin Dance Company brings years of professional training, elaborate costumes, and perfectly choreographed routines that have dazzled audiences across Europe.

In comparison, these local ponies spend their days carrying tourists along beach trails. Though the children's determination to save their riding centre is touching, this David versus Goliath matchup seems decidedly one-sided."

Silence fell in the tack room. Ella's shoulders slumped as she re-read the words.

"Maybe they're right," she said quietly, her voice trembling slightly.

"We're just kids with regular ponies. The Dublin dancers have proper training, fancy costumes, everything."

"All those hours of practice..." Finn added, shaking his head.

"But how can we possibly compete with professionals who do this for a living?"

Olivia stared at the newspaper, her throat tight. They had worked so hard, put in countless hours of practice, even learned historical riding techniques. But now, faced with the reality of their competition, doubt crept in like a cold fog.

Was this really the end of the Killgregory Trekking Centre and their ponies?

Chapter 11

The morning sun was just peeking over the horizon as Olivia gave Daisy one final brush, the pony's grey coat gleaming like polished silver. Since their interview on the radio, the local newspaper had come to talk with them too.

The reporter had been nice enough, and the article had praised their efforts but doubted they would win. Still, the children had doubled their efforts, determined to prove the newspaper wrong.

"There you go, girl," Olivia murmured, running her hand down Daisy's neck. The pony turned her head to nuzzle Olivia's pocket, searching for treats.

"Not now, silly billy. We need to keep your face clean!"

The pony's tack sat ready nearby. They had spent hours the previous evening cleaning every piece of leather until they could see their reflections in it.

In the next stable, Ella was plaiting Rose's mane with careful precision, frowning slightly in concentration as she wove the strands together. The dun pony stood patiently, occasionally shifting her weight but staying remarkably still for the careful work. Finn had already finished preparing Snowy, who was absolutely spotless with not a grassy or muddy patch to be seen on his body.

Ms. O'Leary bustled around her ancient horse lorry, going through her usual pre-journey checks.

The old vehicle had seen better days. Its once-shiny blue paint now dulled and chipped with age, and the aluminium sides bore the battle scars of countless journeys. But like an old friend, it had always been reliable, carrying precious pony cargo safely to shows and events across Ireland for the past twenty years.

"Right then," she called out cheerfully, her voice carrying across the yard where the three kids were making final preparations with their ponies.

"Let's start loading up! We need to leave in thirty minutes to make it to Cork on time."

Ms. O'Leary looked at the lorry, ticking items off her mental checklist. The tires looked good, oil levels were fine, and she'd topped up the fuel yesterday. Everything seemed in order, though the lorry's familiar creaks and groans reminded her of its advancing age. Still, Ms. O'Leary patted its worn side affectionately - this trusty vehicle had never let her down before.

Nearby, Daisy, Rose, and Snowy stood perfectly groomed, their coats gleaming in the morning light. Their tack had been cleaned until it shone, and carefully packed show outfits hung in protective bags nearby.

The excitement of the upcoming performance was palpable. Everyone had turned out to see them off and wish them good luck. As she stepped out onto the yard, Olivia realized other riders at the centre were rooting for them, too, hoping they could save the day.

One little girl who rode most Saturdays gave her a little wave and Olivia smiled back at her.

They began the familiar routine of loading the ponies, each one walking calmly up the ramp into the lorry.

Daisy went first, her hooves making hollow sounds on the metal ramp. Rose followed without hesitation, and finally Snowy, all three settling into their traveling positions with the ease of experienced travellers.

Everything was going according to plan - until Ms. O'Leary tried to close the back ramp of the horse lorry.

There was an ominous creaking sound, followed by a sharp crack that seemed to echo through the entire yard. The ramp wouldn't close properly, hanging at an awkward angle that made everyone's hearts sink.

"Oh no," Ms. O'Leary whispered, her face draining of colour. She tried again, pulling harder, but the ramp wouldn't budge.

"The hinge has completely broken. It's sheared right through."

Olivia felt her stomach drop as she watched Ms. O'Leary inspect the damage. The metal hinge had rusted through over the years, finally giving way at the worst possible moment. Without a properly closing ramp, there was no way they could safely transport the ponies to Cork.

"Can we fix it?" Finn asked desperately, moving closer to examine the broken hinge.

Ms. O'Leary shook her head, her voice tight with worry.

"This needs welding work. Even if we could find someone to do it on a Saturday morning, it would take hours to repair properly."

She checked her watch, her expression growing more concerned.

"The competition starts in three hours. We'd never make it in time."

Ella slumped against Daisy's neck, tears welling in her eyes.

"After all our hard work... we can't even get there."

All their practice, all their hopes of saving the trekking centre, stopped by a broken hinge on the morning of the competition.

"But... but we have to get to Cork!" Ella's voice cracked with panic, her hands still holding Rose's lead rope.

"The show starts in three hours!"

Finn ran his hands through his curly hair in frustration, pacing back and forth.

"Can we fix it temporarily? Maybe with some rope or wire or something?"

Ms. O'Leary shook her head slowly, her expression grave.

"This needs proper welding. We can't transport horses with an unsecured ramp - it's not safe. One wrong move and..."

She didn't finish the sentence, but they all understood the implications.

Olivia felt as if all the air had been sucked out of her lungs. After everything they'd been through, all the practice, all the preparation, all the early mornings and late evenings - they were going to fail because of a broken hinge?

She watched as Daisy poked her head out of the lorry, looking at them curiously with her kind eyes, and felt tears welling up in her eyes.

"There has to be another way," she said desperately, looking around at their small group. Her voice wavered but grew stronger with determination.

"We can't give up now. We just can't. Not after everything we've done to get here."

The silence that followed was deafening as reality sank in. Without transport, they couldn't get to Cork. Without getting to Cork, they couldn't compete. Without competing, they couldn't win the prize money. Without the prize money...

The future of Killgregory Trekking Centre, and their beloved ponies seemed to be slipping away with each passing minute, like sand through their fingers.

Chapter 12

The yard fell silent except for the occasional pawing of hooves and soft nickering of the ponies. Ms. O'Leary stood looking at the broken lorry ramp, her brow furrowed in thought as she absently patted the vehicle's worn blue panels. Suddenly, her face brightened with the spark of an idea.

"Wait a minute," she said, pulling her mobile phone from her pocket.

“I have an idea. Let me try something."

She took out her mobile phone, walked a few steps away toward the office, and made a call, speaking quietly into the phone with an urgency in her voice that made the children strain to hear.

Olivia, Ella, and Finn huddled near the lorry, trying to comfort each other while catching fragments of Ms. O'Leary's conversation. Daisy reached out from her partition, nudging Olivia gently as if sensing her rider's distress. The grey pony's coat gleamed from their careful grooming, making the situation feel even more heart breaking. They were so prepared, so ready for their big moment.

"It'll be okay," Ella whispered, though her voice trembled slightly.

She reached up to scratch Rose's nose through the partition, the dun pony's freshly plaited mane a testament to their morning's work.

“It just has to be.”

Finn paced back and forth, his boots scuffing against the gravel as he glanced repeatedly between Ms. O'Leary and the broken ramp. Snowy watched his movements with interest, occasionally nickering softly as if trying to reassure his young rider.

"That was Lucy Mulcahy," Ms. O'Leary announced, returning with a broad smile.

"She's offered to help! She'll be here in ten minutes with her lorry."

"Lucy Mulcahy? Are you serious?" Ella's eyes widened.

"Yes. She has a new lorry that will be perfect to get us all to Cork in time," Ms. O'Leary nodded.

"She's just finishing up her morning feed and heading straight over. Quick now, let's get the ponies back into their stables while we wait. We'll need to move fast once she arrives!"

With help from the crowd, they braced the ramp just in case, carefully unloading the ponies and leading them back to their stables.

The morning sun climbed higher in the sky, reminding them of the ticking clock. Every minute counted if they were going to make it to Cork in time, and every second felt like an eternity.

Soon, though, they heard the rumble of an engine, and Lucy's smart new lorry appeared at the yard entrance. It was a far cry from Ms. O'Leary's old blue one.

This lorry was gleaming white with professional lettering along the sides advertising "Mulcahy Eventing." A gold horse appearing to take off as if to jump the letters painted beside the words.

Lucy jumped down from the cab, her blonde hair tied back in a neat ponytail.

"Right then," she said briskly, but with a kind smile.

"Let's get you lot to Cork! We've no time to waste."

Working together, they quickly transferred all their equipment, tack and show gear into Lucy's lorry. Lucy's horse lorry was spotlessly clean and much more spacious than Ms. O'Leary's old lorry. It even had sleeping quarters and a kitchen! One by one, they led the ponies up the ramp - Daisy first, then Rose, and finally Snowy. This time, the ramp closed smoothly and securely.

"All aboard!" Lucy called out cheerfully, holding the passenger door open. The three kids and Ms. O'Leary climbed in, squeezing into the luxurious cab that still smelled new.

As they pulled out of the yard, Olivia looked back at Ms. O'Leary's broken lorry, now sitting forlornly in the morning sun. The small crowd of hopeful Trekking Centre patrons waved them on. She glanced at Lucy, who was humming quietly as she drove and felt a wave of gratitude wash over her.

"Thank you so much for helping us," Olivia said softly from her seat behind Lucy, her voice full of gratitude.

She glanced at Daisy on the little video camera on Lucy's dashboard. The grey pony was traveling contentedly in the spacious lorry.

"We thought all our hard work was going to waste this morning."

Lucy smiled warmly, keeping her eyes on the winding coastal road ahead.

"That's what neighbours are for. Besides," she added with a knowing look in the rearview mirror, "I wouldn't want you to miss your chance to show everyone what Kerry Connemara ponies can do! You know, I learnt on a Conny."

“Really?” Ella asked.

Lucy nodded.

"Yep, my first pony. Concord," she smiled. "He thought he was as fast as a jet plane, too," she giggled, and Olivia smiled.

The journey to Cork passed in a blur of nervous excitement and quiet anticipation. Lucy entertained them with stories of her youth riding Concord and competition experiences, including tales of near-disasters turned triumphs that had them all laughing and feeling more optimistic about their last-minute transport crisis.

"I remember my first big competition," Lucy shared, navigating a roundabout with practiced ease.

"My horse threw a shoe an hour before we were due to compete. I thought it was all over, but a kind farrier stepped in and saved the day. Sometimes a disaster can turn out OK in the end!"

Ms. O'Leary nodded from the passenger seat, adding, "And they make for great stories afterward!"

"Isn't that the truth," Lucy laughed.

Ella and Finn sat quietly in the back, occasionally checking their phones for the time, while Olivia watched the familiar Kerry landscape gradually change as they headed south. The rolling hills gave way to more urban surroundings, and finally, the outskirts of Cork city came into view through the morning mist.

The steady rhythm of the lorry and the occasional quiet nickering of the ponies created a soothing backdrop to their journey, helping to calm their pre-show nerves as they drew closer to their destination and the biggest performance of their lives.

"Look!" Finn pointed through the windscreen. "There's the show grounds!"

Lucy skillfully manoeuvred the lorry through the busy showground entrance, following the signs for competitor parking. They had made it - and with just enough time to spare.

As they began unloading the ponies, Olivia caught sight of the main arena where they would be performing.

Her heart started beating faster, but this time it wasn't from worry, it was from excitement. Thanks to Lucy's kindness and quick thinking, their chance to save the trekking centre was still alive.

Now they just had to prove that three ordinary trekking ponies from Kerry could compete with the best of them.

Chapter 13

The backstage area of Cork & Kerry's Top Talent Show buzzed with nervous energy. Performers of all kinds hurried back and forth, dancers stretching in colourful costumes, musicians tuning their instruments, and even a juggler practicing with glittering pins. Among this creative chaos, three kids and their Connemara ponies waited their turn.

Olivia ran her hands over Daisy's neck, the familiar feel of the pony's sleek coat helping to calm her nerves. The grey mare stood perfectly still, seemingly unfazed by the bright lights, unusual environment, and the occasional bursts of music from the main arena.

Then again, Olivia thought, she had time travelled to France and Pluvinel's academy. Next to them, Ella was double-checking Rose's plaits while Finn adjusted Snowy's saddle for the third time.

"Remember," Ms. O'Leary said softly, gathering them into a small circle, "you've practiced this routine lots of times. Your ponies know exactly what to do. Just trust them, and trust yourselves."

Lucy, who had stayed to support them, added with a warm smile, "And remember to breathe! Half the battle is staying calm."

“Oh, and one more thing," Ms. O'Leary smiled.

"No matter what happens, I am so very proud of you."

A stage manager with a clipboard hurried past, calling out, "Connemara pony display team, you're on in twenty minutes!"

"Twenty minutes?" Finn's eyes widened.

"I need to get my riding hat!" He turned toward their gear, then stopped suddenly, his face draining of colour.

"Where's my hat? I can't find my hat!"

The peaceful atmosphere shattered as panic set in. Without an approved riding hat, Finn couldn't perform, and without all three riders, their carefully choreographed routine would fall apart.

"I know I packed it!" Finn's voice cracked with worry as he rummaged through their equipment.

"It was right here with everything else!"

Ella joined the search, checking behind props and under saddle pads. Olivia kept Daisy steady while scanning the area with increasingly worried eyes. Ms. O'Leary and Lucy split up, methodically checking different sections of the backstage area.

"When did you last see it?" Olivia asked, trying to keep her voice calm despite the rising tension.

"When we were unloading!" Finn replied, now close to tears.

"I'm sure I brought it in with everything else!"

"The lorry!" Lucy suddenly exclaimed.

"Let's check there. Sometimes things slip under the horse rugs during the journey."

They rushed to the parking area where Lucy's lorry stood. Time was ticking away, it was just fifteen minutes until their performance. Lucy quickly unlocked the lorry while Finn scrambled inside, pushing aside the horse rugs they'd used during transport.

"Found it!" His triumphant shout echoed from inside the lorry. He emerged clutching his riding hat, his face glowing with relief.

"It was under the horse rugs, just like Lucy said!"

Lucy smiled. "Not my first rodeo."

Racing back to the backstage area, they arrived just as the stage manager returned.

"Ten minutes Connemara pony team! Are you ready?"

Olivia looked at her friends, at their ponies standing patiently nearby, and at Ms. O'Leary and Lucy who had helped them get this far.

She thought about all they'd been through, the early morning practices, the newspaper criticism, the broken lorry, and now the missing hat. Yet here they were, still standing, still ready to show everyone what they could do.

"We're ready," she said firmly, and she meant it. The nervous butterflies were still there in her stomach, but now they felt more like excitement than fear. Next on stage was the Dublin Irish dancing team.

"Look who's here from the Kerry bog," came a sharp voice behind them. Three girls in elaborately embroidered dance costumes and perfectly curled wigs stood watching them, their arms crossed.

The tallest one, who appeared to be their leader, looked at the Kerry kids with barely concealed disdain. Her emerald green costume sparkled under the backstage lights, catching every movement as she shifted her weight with practiced grace.

"The Dublin Irish Dancing Champions don't usually have to compete against pony acts," she continued, her voice dripping with condescension. Her two companions flanked her like perfectly matched bookends, their identical costumes and matching sneers making them look like clones.

"We've won every competition we've entered so far this year," another of the dancers added, adjusting her sparkly tiara with manicured fingers. Her wig bounced with each practiced head tilt as she spoke.

"No offense, but you might want to prepare yourselves for disappointment. This isn't some little country show, you know."

The third dancer snickered, eyeing their simple riding outfits with an exaggerated up-and-down look.

"At least your ponies are clean. That's something, I suppose." She wrinkled her nose as if catching a whiff of something unpleasant.

"Though I can still smell the stables from here."

Olivia felt her cheeks burn hot with anger and embarrassment. She glanced down at her neat but plain show jacket and jodhpurs, suddenly feeling very small compared to their glittering costumes and perfectly styled appearance.

The familiar scent of leather and horses that usually gave her comfort now made her feel self-conscious.

But before she could respond, she felt Ella's hand tighten around hers, a gentle reminder of everything they'd overcome to get here. Finn moved closer too, standing shoulder to shoulder with his friends. They didn't need fancy costumes or perfectly styled hair, they had something much more special: three amazing ponies and months of hard work behind them.

Looking at the dancers' smug faces, Olivia lifted her chin slightly. They didn't need to prove anything to these girls. Their ponies and their performance would speak for themselves. After all, Daisy, Rose, and Snowy had already shown them that sometimes the most extraordinary talents come in the most ordinary packages.

"Places everyone!" the stage manager called out, clipboard in hand as she hurried down the backstage corridor. Her headset crackled with activity while she gestured urgently to the Dublin dance team.

"You're up next!"

The six dancers from Dublin, dressed in elaborate emerald green costumes adorned with Celtic designs, gathered near the stage entrance. Their sequins sparkled under the harsh backstage lighting as they performed their final stretches. Their team captain, a tall girl with perfectly curled hair, threw one last dismissive look at Olivia, Ella, and Finn.

"Good luck with your pony act," she said, her voice dripping with fake sweetness.

"Try not to fall off in front of everyone." Her teammates giggled behind their hands.

Before any of them could respond, the stage manager's voice cut through the tension.

"OK ladies, let's go!" She raised her hand, counting down with her fingers. "In 3, 2, 1 and go!"

The dancers burst onto the stage in perfect formation, as the first notes of traditional Irish music filled the arena. The sound of thunderous applause followed their entrance, making Olivia's stomach twist with nerves as she watched from the wings.

Through the curtain, she could see the packed audience, the judges' table, and the bright stage lights that would soon be shining on them and their ponies.

The enormity of what they were about to do suddenly felt overwhelming.

Chapter 14

The rhythmic sound of the Irish jig filled the backstage area as the Dublin dancers performed. Despite their earlier attitude, Olivia couldn't help but be impressed by their skill. Their movements were perfectly synchronized, their emerald costumes creating mesmerizing patterns as they spun and leaped in perfect unison. The audience's enthusiastic applause and cheers grew louder with each complex sequence.

Ella shifted nervously beside Rose, adjusting her stock tie for the hundredth time.

"They're really good," she whispered, her voice barely audible over the music.

"They are," Finn agreed, absently patting Snowy's neck.

"But we're good too - just different."

His voice carried more confidence than his slightly pale face suggested.

Olivia watched from backstage as the dancers executed a particularly challenging series of steps that had the audience clapping along. The spotlights caught their tiaras and elaborate costumes, sending sparkles across the stage like shooting stars.

Ms. O'Leary placed a reassuring hand on Olivia's shoulder.

"Remember what makes our act special," she said softly.

"It's not just about the performance. It's about the connection between you and your ponies. That's something those dancers, as talented as they are, can't match."

Lucy nodded in agreement.

"And don't forget, you're not just representing yourselves, you're showing everyone what Kerry

Connemara ponies can do. That's worth more than all the sequins in Ireland."

The music swelled to its final crescendo as the Dublin dancers executed a series of perfectly synchronized leaps and turns. Their emerald costumes caught the spotlight, sending sparkles across the arena as they moved with practiced precision.

The lead dancer completed a spectacular solo, her feet moving so quickly they seemed to barely touch the ground. As the last note rang out, all six dancers struck their final pose - heads held high, arms gracefully positioned, and not a curl out of place in their elaborate wigs.

The audience erupted in thunderous applause, with several people rising to their feet. Even Olivia had to admit they were incredible, despite their earlier unkindness backstage.

The dancers exited the stage with practiced grace as the lights dimmed, their faces flushed with exertion and triumph. As they passed by the waiting pony team, they exchanged knowing looks and satisfied smirks.

"Beat that," the lead dancer whispered as she swept past, her tiara glinting under the backstage lights. Her teammates followed, their giggles echoing in the wings as they disappeared toward their dressing room, leaving behind the lingering scent of hairspray and the sound of their clicking shoes.

The stage manager appeared beside them, adjusting her headset.

"Connemara pony display team, you're up next! The stage team have got the sand surface ready for you and your ponies. Places everyone!"

"We're good too," Finn replied firmly, though his hands trembled slightly as he double-checked Snowy's girth.

"Just... different."

Olivia pressed her face against Daisy's neck, drawing comfort from the pony's familiar warmth and sweet hay-scented coat. The grey mare stood calmly, her ears pricked forward with interest at the sounds coming from the stage, but otherwise completely relaxed.

Ms. O'Leary stepped forward, giving each of them a quick hug.

"Remember everything we practiced. Trust your ponies, trust yourselves."

With an encouraging smile, Lucy added, "Show them what Connemara ponies can do!"

Ms. O'Leary gave Finn a leg up onto Snowy as Olivia and Ella mounted. Olivia took a deep breath, checking Daisy's girth one final time. The pony's grey coat gleamed under the backstage lights, her plaited mane neat and perfect. Beside them, Rose and Snowy stood quietly, their coats gleaming, a testament to hours of careful preparation. This is it, she thought.

"In position!" the stage manager called. The three friends exchanged glances; years of friendship and weeks of practice condensed into that single moment of understanding. Together, they walked to the entrance.

"Good luck," Ms. O'Leary whispered as she stepped back.

The stage manager raised her hand, counting down.

"In three..."

Olivia gathered her reins, feeling Daisy's steady presence beneath her.

"Two..."

Ella and Finn moved into position on either side.

"One..."

The lights began to rise.

Chapter 15

The arena lights blazed to life as traditional Irish music filled the air. Olivia guided Daisy forward, the pony's hooves making no sound on the sand surface. To her left and right, Ella and Finn moved in perfect synchronization, their ponies' strides matching Daisy's as they entered the stage in a perfect line.

The audience fell silent, perhaps surprised to see three children and their ponies where they might have expected more dancers or musicians. But as the trio began their carefully choreographed routine, the silence transformed into something else - anticipation.

Moving as one, they performed a series of synchronized circles, their ponies' movements flowing like water. Daisy responded to Olivia's lightest touch, transitioning smoothly from walk to trot, her grey coat shimmering under the stage lights. Rose and Snowy matched her stride for stride, creating patterns that seemed to dance with the music.

Olivia could feel Daisy's enthusiasm growing as they moved into more complex figures. The mare's ears flicked back and forth, catching her rider's subtle cues while staying perfectly in time with the other ponies. They performed shoulder-in along the edge of the stage, the ponies' bodies bent gracefully as they moved sideways and forward simultaneously, staying focused despite the crowd and the lights.

The music shifted, and so did their formation. They separated, each taking a different part of the stage. This was the moment they'd practiced countless times, the individual displays that would showcase each pony's special talents. Ella and Rose performed a series of perfectly balanced turns on the forehand, while Finn and Snowy demonstrated smooth transitions between collected and extended trot.

Olivia and Daisy moved into their solo section, a series of movements performed with one hand on the reins, the other held gracefully to the side. Daisy responded to each subtle shift of Olivia's weight, turning and moving as if reading her mind. In that moment, all nervousness disappeared. It was just a girl and her pony, moving as one, sharing the joy of what they could achieve together.

The three pairs came back together for the finale, cantering together in perfect formation. Their ponies' strides matched exactly, creating a living carousel of light grey, dun, and dapple white. As the music reached its crescendo, they performed one final figure, a synchronized halt at centre stage, the ponies standing perfectly still as the last note faded away.

For a moment, complete silence filled the arena. Then, like a wave breaking on the shore, applause erupted from every corner.

The audience rose to their feet, their cheers echoing off the walls. Olivia could see faces in the crowd, smiling and clapping, some wiping away tears, and a smile spread across her face. She glanced over at Ella and Finn, who were also grinning.

From the wings, Ms. O'Leary beamed with pride, while Lucy gave them a thumbs-up. Even the stage manager was clapping, her clipboard temporarily forgotten.

Olivia leaned forward as they rode off the stage to rub Daisy's neck.

"Good girl," she whispered, her voice thick with emotion.

"The very best girl."

They had done everything they could. Now all they could do was wait for the judges' decision. But somehow, as they led their ponies back to the backstage area, the results didn't seem quite as important anymore. They had shown everyone what their Connemara ponies could do.

In the wings, they could see the Dublin dancers watching their performance from the shadows, their sequined costumes still catching stray beams of light.

Their expressions had transformed from earlier smugness to a mixture of surprise and reluctant admiration. When their leader caught Olivia's eye, she gave a small but definite nod - not quite friendly, but definitely respect. The gesture spoke volumes, acknowledging that perhaps there was more than one way to create magic on stage.

Ms. O'Leary gathered them into a group hug as soon as they dismounted, careful not to dirty their show jackets.

"I am so proud of you all," she said, her voice wavering slightly with emotion.

"The way you handled those complicated dressage movements, how you supported each other through the whole routine - no matter what happens next, you've already won in my book."

Her eyes glistened as she looked at each of them in turn.

Lucy joined them, her face glowing with enthusiasm as she helped them lead the ponies back to their waiting area.

"That was absolutely beautiful!" she exclaimed, patting each pony in turn.

"The way you worked together, the harmony with your ponies, it was just magical! Those shoulder-ins were perfect, and the way you executed those turns on the forehand. I've seen professional riders who couldn't do better."

Daisy, Rose, and Snowy stood quietly nearby, their coats still gleaming under the backstage lights, looking remarkably unruffled despite their complex performance. Each pony seemed to sense their riders' excitement, their ears pricked forward attentively as the children praised and patted them.

The stage manager appeared, still clutching her ever-present clipboard as her headset crackled with backstage chatter. Her professional demeanour softened as she approached the group, who were busy praising their ponies after their performance. Daisy, Rose, and Snowy stood contentedly munching on well-deserved apple treats while their young riders patted their necks with trembling hands.

"The judges will announce the results in thirty minutes," she informed them, pausing to adjust her headset as someone's voice buzzed through. After a quick "Copy that" into her microphone, she turned back to the group with a warm smile that crinkled the corners of her eyes.

"That was quite something, kids. I've been stage managing this show for five years, and I've never seen anything quite like it."

She shook her head in amazement, watching as the ponies continued to stand calmly despite the bustling backstage environment.

"The way those ponies moved together, like they were dancing! And so well-behaved too. Most acts I deal with are either singers or dancers. But your ponies..."

She gestured appreciatively toward the three Connemaras.

"Quite something indeed. They're real professionals, aren't they?"

The genuine praise in her voice made Olivia, Ella, and Finn beam with pride, their earlier nervousness temporarily forgotten as they exchanged excited glances.

Even Ms. O'Leary and Lucy were smiling broadly at the unexpected compliment. Now they just had to wait and see if they had done enough to save the trekking stables.

Chapter 16

The backstage area hummed with nervous energy as competitors gathered to hear the results. The air felt thick with anticipation, filled with the mingled scents of horse, hairspray, and nervous excitement. Olivia's heart pounded so loudly she was sure everyone could hear it.

Daisy seemed to sense her anxiety, gently nudging her rider's shoulder with her soft muzzle. The pony's familiar warmth and sweet hay-scented breath helped calm Olivia's racing thoughts.

She glanced around at the other contestants, all nervously awaiting their fate: the Dublin Dancers in their sparkly dresses, the juggler, his pins tucked under his arm, and a myriad of singers and comedians. Ella nudged her arm and she realized that the announcer had stepped out onto the stage.

"And now," the announcer's voice boomed through the speakers, echoing off the walls of the packed auditorium, "the moment we've all been waiting for. Our judges have made their decision."

Ella grabbed Olivia's hand on one side while Finn took her other, their palms slightly sweaty with nerves. Ms. O'Leary and Lucy stood behind them, Lucy adjusting her show jacket buttons, a nervous habit she'd developed during her competition days, while Ms. O'Leary stood perfectly still, her face a mixture of hope and pride.

The stage lights altered, and someone started playing a drumroll somewhere, making Olivia's heart beat even faster.

The Dublin dancers stood nearby, their sequins catching the light as they waited with barely contained anticipation.

Their earlier smugness had been replaced by genuine tension. The lead dancer kept smoothing her already-perfect costume while her teammates whispered among themselves, stealing glances at the pony display team.

Around them, other competitors shifted restlessly. The stage lights shifted again, casting long shadows across the floor. Olivia could barely take the tension that seemed to last forever. Only the gentle sounds of the ponies, a soft nicker here, a moved hoof there, soothed her nerves.

Daisy, Rose, and Snowy stood quietly together, their well-groomed coats still gleaming despite the performance, seemingly unaffected by the tension that gripped their young riders.

The stage manager appeared briefly in the wings, her headset crackling with activity as she gave last-minute instructions to her crew. She caught Olivia's eye and gave her a quick thumbs-up before disappearing back into the controlled chaos of backstage operations.

"In third place..." the announcer paused dramatically,

"The marching band from the Kerry School of Music!"

Polite applause filled the arena, along with a few whoops from the group's supporters, as the band of delighted musicians stepped forward to accept their trophy, waving at the crowd.

"In second place..."

Another pause that seemed to last forever. "The Dublin Dance Academy!"

There was a slight murmur amongst the crowd as the favourites to win were announced in second place. The dancers in their emerald costumes moved forward, their disappointment visible despite their professional smiles. As they passed by, their leader caught Olivia's eye and gave her a slight nod of acknowledgment.

"And now, ladies and gentlemen, our first place winners of Cork & Kerry's Top Talent Show, with their unique blend of horsemanship, artistry, and Irish heritage...

...The Killgregory Connemara Pony Display Team!"

For a moment, Olivia couldn't move. Had she heard correctly? Then Ella was squealing, Finn was jumping up and down, and Ms. O'Leary was wiping tears from her eyes.

"You did it!" Lucy exclaimed, hugging each of them in turn.

"You actually did it!"

The stage manager hurried over to them, her headset crackling with activity.

"The announcer wants the Connemara pony team back on stage in five minutes for the prize-giving ceremony," she said, checking her clipboard.

"In the meantime, Tommy O'Sullivan from Kerry will be performing his newest song."

Through the wings, they could hear the local singer's melodic voice filling the arena, accompanied by the gentle strum of an acoustic guitar. The familiar Kerry accent in his lyrics brought smiles to their faces as they prepared their ponies for one final appearance.

"Better check those plaits one last time," Ms. O'Leary suggested, helping them tidy their ponies' manes.

"We want them looking their absolute best for the presentation."

The ponies stood quietly, seeming to understand the importance of the moment. Daisy's grey coat still gleamed under the backstage lights, while Rose and

Snowy looked equally pristine despite their earlier performance.

DJ Declan from Kerry South West Radio rushed forward with his microphone, his face flushed with excitement as he weaved through the backstage crowd. His trademark red headphones hung around his neck, and his eyes sparkled with the thrill of capturing this moment for his listeners.

"This is incredible!" he exclaimed, holding the microphone out while simultaneously adjusting his portable broadcasting equipment.

"We've just announced that you've won live on radio, and I've just received word that the entire village of Killgregory is celebrating in the streets! Mrs. Murphy at the post office says people are dancing outside the pub, and old Tommy O'Brien is playing his fiddle on Main Street! Even the fishing boats in the harbour are sounding their horns!"

He paused to catch his breath, then continued with growing enthusiasm.

"I'm told they could hear the cheering all the way to the lighthouse! Tell us, how does it feel to know you've not only won the competition but brought such joy to your entire community?"

His words tumbled out in a rush of genuine excitement, the radio personality's usual smooth delivery forgotten in the emotion of the moment. The small red light on his recording equipment blinked steadily, broadcasting every word back to the eagerly listening residents of Kerry.

Olivia looked at her friends, then at their beloved ponies.

"It feels like a dream," she managed to say.

"But we couldn't have done it without our ponies. They're the real stars."

"And this means the trekking centre is saved?" DJ Declan prompted.

Ms. O'Leary stepped forward, her voice thick with emotion.

"We hope so; we'll at least be able to stay open until the council comes up with enough money to repair the bridge to Killgregory Castle. Then our historic treks can continue, and these wonderful ponies will keep sharing their home at Killgregory with visitors for years to come."

“Well, I don’t think you’ll need the council,” DJ Declan announced. Olivia frowned.

“Because, and this is just coming in to me from one of our news team, that several big donations have been made to sort the bridge out after seeing the performance of these amazing young people and their ponies.”

“What?” Olivia looked over at Ella and Finn. “Really?”

“That’s amazing!” Ella gasped.

"So far, I'm hearing that the total donated to the repair fund is more than thirty thousand euros!"

“Thirty thousand?” Ms. O’Leary’s eyes went wide. “That’ll easily fix the bridge.”

"Looks like you might get the lorry fixed and the bridge done," Lucy smiled.

As photographers' flashes went off around them, Olivia buried her face in Daisy's mane, breathing in the familiar scent of pony and victory.

They had done it. They had done it. The trekking centre was saved, and they had shown everyone just how special Connemara ponies could be.

Chapter 17

The familiar Irish music began to play once more as Olivia, Ella, and Finn rode their ponies back onto the brightly lit stage. The audience erupted in applause, even louder than before. Under the dazzling lights, Olivia could see hundreds of faces beaming up at them, and there, in the third row, were her parents.

Her mother was dabbing her eyes with a tissue while her father stood tall, clapping with obvious pride.

"Look at your mum and dad!" Ella whispered excitedly as they rode forward.

"I think your mum's crying!"

"So is mine!" Finn added with a grin, nodding toward another section of the audience where his parents were waving enthusiastically.

The ponies moved perfectly in step, their hooves making hardly any sound on the sand as they approached centre stage where a giant trophy and an oversized cheque waited. The trophy caught the stage lights, sending sparkles dancing across the arena, while the cheque's large numbers, €10,000, seemed almost unreal.

"Ladies and gentlemen," the announcer's voice boomed, "please welcome back our champions - the Killgregory Connemara Pony Display Team!"

Ms. O'Leary stepped forward to accept the cheque, her voice wavering with emotion as she spoke into the microphone.

"Thank you all so much. These children and their wonderful ponies have shown what can be achieved with dedication, hard work, and most importantly, kindness to our four-legged partners." She paused, holding up the cheque with trembling hands.

"This money means everything to our little trekking centre. Along with some very kind and generous donations, we'll be able to repair the historic bridge to Killgregory Castle, preserving not just our business but also a cherished piece of Kerry's heritage. Our Connemara ponies can continue carrying visitors along the ancient paths, sharing the magic of our coastline with generations to come. These three young riders and their amazing ponies haven't just won a competition - they've helped save a tradition that goes back hundreds of years."

The pride in her voice was unmistakable as she gestured to Olivia, Ella, and Finn, who sat tall on their ponies under the bright stage lights.

"Thanks to them, the hoofbeats of Connemara ponies will continue to echo across the parish of Killgregory, just as they have for generations. I couldn't be more proud of what these children and their remarkable ponies have accomplished today."

Olivia's gaze swept across the crowd as they lined up their ponies.

For just a moment, among the sea of modern clothes and familiar faces, she caught sight of something unusual. A gentleman in a snug, red fitted padded doublet, dark breeches, and black leather riding boots, his bearing noble and proud.

He stood out from the crowd like a figure from another time, and as their eyes met, he gave her a gentle, knowing smile. Antoine de Pluvinel's kind eyes twinkled with approval, and he gave a small, elegant bow. When Olivia blinked, he was gone, leaving her wondering if she had even seen him at all or if it had only been her imagination.

The presenter's voice booming through the microphone as he praised their unique performance and the grace of their Connemara ponies. But Olivia was still thinking about that glimpse of Pluvinel.

Had he really been there, watching their display of gentle horsemanship? Had he seen how they'd used his teachings of patience and understanding to create something beautiful?

Daisy shifted beneath her, bringing Olivia back to the present moment. The pony's ears were pricked forward, taking in the applause with quiet dignity. Olivia leaned forward to pat her neck, whispering, "You would have made Monsieur de Pluvinel proud, my friend."

As the lights dimmed and the music faded, Olivia knew that whether real or imagined, Pluvinel's spirit had been with them throughout their journey. She guided Daisy toward the exit, flanked by Ella on Rose and Finn on Snowy, their faces glowing with joy and triumph. The ponies' hooves made soft thuds against the arena surface as they walked in perfect formation one final time.

Lucy was waiting for them in the wings, practically bouncing with excitement.

"That was absolutely magnificent!" she exclaimed as they dismounted.

"The way you rode out there - such poise, such harmony with your ponies." Her eyes sparkled as she helped them lead their ponies back to the preparation area.

"You've shown everyone what real horsemanship looks like. Not just tricks and fancy moves, but true partnership with your ponies."

The three friends exchanged delighted grins, still buzzing from their victory and the thunderous applause that had followed them off stage. Their ponies stood contentedly beside them, ears pricked forward, seeming to understand they had been part of something very special.

Chapter 18

The spring sunshine sparkled off the lake at Killgregory Castle as the sound of construction equipment filled the air. A yellow digger and large red crane were visible working at the ancient stone bridge, where a small team of builders moved purposefully among the scaffolding.

The work to restore the historic crossing had already begun, with the old stones being meticulously cleaned and reset, while new supporting steel structure was added beneath to ensure the bridge would stand strong for generations to come.

"It's looking great already!" called out Mike O'Connor, one of the lead builders, as he spotted Olivia, Ella, and Finn approaching.

He climbed down from his perch on the scaffolding, his weathered face breaking into a broad smile.

"We've been following your story in the local paper. My wife had it playing live on the radio when you won, we couldn't believe our ears!"

He wiped his hands on his hi-vis vest before continuing.

"You've done something really special here, saving the trekking centre. My own little ones are only toddlers now, but I've already told the missus I want them to learn to ride here when they're old enough. There's something magical about this spot, with the castle and the lake, and I can't think of a better place for children to learn about Connemara ponies."

The kids beamed with pride as Mike explained how they were incorporating modern engineering while preserving the bridge's historic character.

"We're keeping all the original stones we can," he said, pointing to where his team was carefully cleaning centuries-old masonry.

"But underneath, we're adding steel reinforcement that'll keep it standing for another few hundred years at least. Best of both worlds, you might say, just like your riding display, never forgetting the old traditions that are proven to work."

The three friends turned their ponies away from the construction site, following the ancient trail that wound through the gorse-covered hills. Daisy's hooves made soft thuds against the worn path, while Rose and Snowy fell into step beside her. The sound of machinery faded behind them, replaced by the gentle whisper of the sea breeze through the grass and the distant cry of seabirds.

"I can't believe how quickly they started work," Ella remarked, adjusting Rose's reins as the pony stretched down for another mouthful of grass.

"Ms. O'Leary says they'll be finished within two weeks," Finn announced, watching the yellow excavator carefully position another massive stone block into place on the ancient bridge.

The spring sunshine glinted off the machinery as workers in hard hats called instructions to each other over the sound of construction.

"Just in time for the summer season," Ella added.

"Did you see all the booking requests on Ms. O'Leary's desk? The phone hasn't stopped ringing since we won!"

Olivia smiled, remembering how the office had been buzzing with activity that morning. The familiar smell of coffee and fresh-baked scones from the kitchen mixed with the excitement in the air.

"The website crashed twice yesterday because so many people were trying to book rides. And did you see? Someone even wrote an article about us in the Irish Daily Times!"

The article had praised their innovative combination of traditional Irish culture and classical dressage, featuring a photo of them performing their winning routine. Ms. O'Leary had already framed it and hung it proudly in the tack room alongside their trophy. The headline read "Young Riders Save Historic Kerry Trekking Centre with Classical Horsemanship."

"Lucy called this morning too," Ella added, adjusting Rose's headcollar.

"She says there's been huge interest in Connemara ponies since our performance. The Irish Connemara Pony Society wants us to do a demonstration at their summer show!"

"A demo," Olivia sighed.

"It still seems so unreal." She glanced back towards the sound of construction.

"Remember when we first started practicing?" Ella laughed.

"We could barely keep in time with each other, let alone the music!"

"And now look at us," Finn said proudly. "Champions!"

They paused on the hill and watched as another truck of building materials wound its way up the castle road. The ancient walls of Killgregory Castle rose behind it, their grey stone gleaming in the sunlight. Soon, riders would once again be able to cross the bridge and circle the castle's base, following the trail that generations of horses and ponies had travelled before them.

"Shall we take the coastal trail?" Olivia suggested, gathering up Daisy's reins.

"One last ride before heading home?"

The others nodded eagerly, and they turned their ponies toward the familiar path that wound along the clifftops. The tide was coming in, sending waves crashing against the rocks below. Seabirds wheeled overhead, their cries carried on the wind as the ponies picked their way carefully along the trail.

"You know," Olivia said thoughtfully as they rode, "I think Monsieur de Pluvinel would have loved this place. The way the ponies have to think for themselves, picking their path carefully, just like he taught about letting horses use their own minds."

"And working in harmony with them instead of forcing them," Ella added, patting Rose's neck affectionately.

"That's what made our display special - we weren't just showing off tricks, we were showing real partnership with our ponies."

They rode in comfortable silence for a while, each lost in their own thoughts as their ponies carried them sure-footedly along the cliff path. The sound of hoofbeats mingled with the crash of waves and the cry of seabirds, creating a peaceful rhythm that seemed as timeless as the ancient castle behind them.

Olivia was thinking about how far they had progressed.

"We have learned so much more than just riding skills. We learned about history, about working together, about trusting our ponies and ourselves."

As they turned for home, the setting sun painted the sky in brilliant shades of pink and gold. Soon the bridge would be complete, and new adventures would begin.

But for now, three friends and their beloved ponies rode happily beside each other, enjoying the company of their famous Connemara ponies.

Chapter 19

A few days later, the familiar pink horse lorry rolled into the yard, its cheerful paint gleaming in the sunlight. Izzy's mobile pony book library had returned to Killgregory, and the sight of it brought smiles to everyone's faces.

Olivia, Ella, and Finn ran over to the lorry, eager to update Izzy on what had happened. The door of the horsebox swung open, and Izzy emerged, her curly blonde hair caught in the sea breeze.

"My champions!" she exclaimed, clapping her hands together in delight.

"I can't believe it! I've been following your story on the radio and in the papers. What an absolutely wonderful achievement!"

She stepped down from the horsebox and gave Olivia, Ella and Finn a warm hug.

"I knew when I first met you that there was something special about you three. The way you connected with those books about classical horsemanship. Not many young riders show such interest in the old masters."

Ms. O'Leary appeared from the tack room, and Izzy turned to greet her with enthusiasm.

"Congratulations on saving this wonderful place," she said warmly.

"It would have been such a shame to lose all this history and tradition. I heard the bridge repairs are coming along beautifully?"

"They certainly are," Ms. O'Leary replied, beaming.

"Would you like to see it? You can actually see the bridge and castle from here." She pointed toward the bridge and distant castle, where the scaffolding was visible in the distance.

"And old blue's been repaired," she smiled over at the trusty old horsebox standing newly repaired in its usual parking place.

Olivia, Ella, and Finn hurried back to the tack room, emerging moments later with their borrowed books clutched in their arms. Olivia carefully handed back the worn copy of Pluvinel's treatise, its leather binding soft from years of careful handling.

"Thank you so much for lending us these," she said earnestly.

"They helped us more than you could know."

"I think I might have some idea," Izzy replied with a mysterious smile that made Olivia wonder just how much the librarian really knew about her adventures.

While Ms. O'Leary and Izzy continued chatting about the bridge restoration, the children began exploring the shelves inside the horsebox. The familiar scent of old books mixed with the leather conditioning oil Izzy used on her collection. Sunlight streamed through the windows, illuminating the carefully organized shelves.

"Look at this one!" Ella exclaimed, pulling out a glossy book about horse care.

"It has everything about grooming and feeding, even natural remedies!"

Finn's eyes lit up when he discovered an original edition of the Duke of Newcastle's famous work on horsemanship.

"Look at these illustrations!" he called to the others, showing them the detailed drawings of classical riding exercises.

Olivia found herself reaching for a colourful paperback about a girl and her pony in New Zealand.

"This looks exciting," she said, flipping through pages filled with descriptions of beach rides and mountain trails.

"As exciting as traveling to France?" Finn whispered, making Olivia smirk.

The three friends exchanged knowing looks as they held their new selections. There was something special about Izzy's traveling library, something that went beyond just books and stories.

Perhaps it was magic, or perhaps it was simply the invaluable wisdom of horsemanship passed down through generations of riders and writers. Whatever it was, the children were glad it visited them.

Soon it was time for Izzy to climb back into her horsebox, and prepare to leave.

"Keep reading, keep learning, and keep loving your ponies," Izzy called out cheerfully as she started the engine of her pink horsebox.

"Because that's where the real magic happens!"

The three friends and Ms. O'Leary stood waving as the distinctive pink library on wheels pulled away, its painted horses and books seeming to dance in the late afternoon sunlight.

"Safe journey, Izzy!" Ms. O'Leary called out.

"And thank you for bringing such wonderful books to inspire our young riders!"

"Goodbye!" Olivia, Ella, and Finn shouted in unison, clutching their newly borrowed books to their chests.

"See you next month!"

They watched until the horsebox disappeared around the bend in the lane, its cheerful pink colour standing out against the green Kerry landscape. The sound of hooves could be heard from the nearby paddock where

Daisy, Rose, and Snowy grazed peacefully, unaware that their young riders were already dreaming of new adventures inspired by the books they held.

"Do you think she knew?" Finn whispered.

"I think some things are better left as mysteries," Ella replied with a smile.

Olivia looked down at her new book, then up at her friends.

"What matters is what we learned - about how amazing our ponies are, about believing in ourselves and saving Killgregory Stables."

Together, they walked back to the stables. The afternoon sun streamed through the stable windows, casting long shadows across the yard, and in the distance, the ancient walls of Killgregory Castle stood proud against the sky, guardian of both past and future adventures.

Antonie de Pluvinel

Antoine de Pluvinel was born in 1552 in Crest, Dauphiné, France. He was a famous French riding master. He is known for his kind and innovative approaches to horsemanship, which greatly influenced modern dressage.

Pluvinel studied in Naples, Italy with Giovanni Battista Pignatelli, before returning to France to teach and serve as a courtier to three French kings: Henry III, Henry IV, and Louis XIII.

Pluvinel founded the "Académie d'Équitation" in 1594 near what is now Place des Pyramides in Paris. This prestigious riding school trained French nobility in horsemanship and other aristocratic skills such as dance, fashion, and mathematics.

At the Hotel Regina Louvre in Paris today, you can see a plaque on the wall which marks the location of where the "Académie d'Équitation" was located. Sadly, Pluvinel's "Académie d'Équitation" is no longer there.

Pluvinel's book, *L'Instruction du Roy en l'exercice de monter à cheval* ("Instruction of the King in the Art of Riding"), was published after he died in 1625. It is considered a cornerstone of equestrian literature. The book emphasizes gentle training methods, including the use of praise and softer bits, contrasting with the harsher techniques of other horse riders and trainers before him.

Antoine de Pluvinel is also famous for introducing techniques such as shoulder-in movements and the use of pillars for horse training. He strongly believed in:

- Using praise to encourage the horse
- Treating horses with kindness and understanding
- Careful application of aids
- Employing softer bits for better communication

- The introduction of three-track movements.

Pluvinel continues to influence riders and trainers in their pursuit of harmony and excellence in equestrian arts today.

Antonie de Pluvinel died on August 24, 1620, but his legacy still lives on.

William Cavendish, 1st Duke of Newcastle

William Cavendish, 1st Duke of Newcastle (c. 16 December 1593 – 25 December 1676), was a prominent English courtier, arts patron, and renowned horseman. Born in Handsworth, South Yorkshire, he was the eldest surviving son of Sir Charles Cavendish and Catherine Ogle. He was elected member of Parliament for East Retford in 1614 and appointed governor of the Prince of Wales in 1638.

William Cavendish studied at Master de Pluvinel's Academy, where he learned the techniques of manège. The skills and knowledge he acquired in Paris greatly influenced his approach to horsemanship.

Riding House built in the 1630s by William Cavendish, at Bolsover Castle in Derbyshire became one of the earliest indoor riding arenas in England to survive intact. It included a large indoor arena for horse training and demonstrations, viewing galleries with raked seating for spectators, stables, a smithy and forge and accommodation for servants and staff.

William Cavendish taught horsemanship at the Riding House from the 1630s onwards and Cavendish used this space to train horses in advanced movements and to demonstrate his expertise in the art of manège. It was here that Cavendish taught the future King Charles II to ride in 1636.

During the English Civil War, Cavendish was a staunch Royalist, financing much of the war effort himself and serving as Royalist Captain-General in Northern England. He was defeated at the Battle of Marston Moor in 1644 and went into exile. After his return from exile in 1660, following the English Civil War, Cavendish continued to use the Riding House at Bolsover Castle.

Cavendish published two horsemanship manuals, one in English and one in French, setting out his new method for the rearing, training and management of the horse, the ancestor of today's dressage horse.

Newcastle's second book, *A New Method, and Extraordinary Invention, to Dress Horses* (London: 1667), was published in English.

Cavendish also built a magnificent riding house at Welbeck Abbey, designed by John Smithson. This riding hall was one of the most significant additions to the estate and reflected Cavendish's passion for horsemanship.

By 1670, William Cavendish, had retired from active political life and devoted himself to his passion for training horses and writing about horsemanship. William Cavendish's legacy extends beyond his political and military roles, with his contributions to horsemanship and dressage remaining influential to this day. Today, Welbeck Abbey remains a private residence with parts of its estate accessible through guided tours.

François Robichon de La Guérinière

François Robichon de La Guérinière (1688–1751) was a French riding master who had a profound effect on accepted methods for horse training, and one of the most influential writers on the art of dressage. Born in Normandy, he became an écuyer du roi (equerry to the king) in 1715 and directed an equestrian academy in Paris for 15 years.

In 1730, De La Guérinière was appointed as the Directeur du Manège des Tuileries (Director of the Tuileries Riding Academy) in Paris. This appointment was made by Prince Charles of Lorraine, the Grand écuyer de France. The Manège des Tuileries was a prestigious institution, originally founded by Antoine de Pluvinel, who had been a riding master to King Louis XIII. La Guérinière managed the Manège des

Tuileries until his death in 1751, a period of about 21 years. During his tenure at the Tuileries, La Guérinière published his famous work "L'École de Cavalerie" (The School of Horsemanship) in 1733, which became a foundational text in classical dressage.

His treatise *L'École de Cavalerie,* "The School of Horsemanship", which was published in parts between 1729 and 1731, and as a complete work in 1733, is an important book on the training of the horse, detailing equitation, veterinary treatment, and general horsemanship.

In his book, de La Guérinière stresses the use of few aids and punishments while riding. He advises the use of the shoulder-in at all gaits, including the gallop.

De La Guérinière states the rider must also have a good seat in order to have a soft, light hand, and makes several references to William Cavendish, 1st Duke of Newcastle.

La Guérinière is credited with several important innovations in equestrian training:

1. Champion of the shoulder-in exercise, which he called the "alpha and omega of all exercises."

2. Development of the flying change and counter-canter.

3. Emphasis on using few aids and punishments while riding.

4. Focus on creating a light, obedient, and calm horse through progressive schooling.

His methods aimed to increase the horse's suppleness and balance, prioritizing natural gaits over artificial movements.

La Guérinière advocated for a more natural and less artificial approach to horsemanship compared to some of his predecessors. He emphasized the importance of understanding horse conformation and working with the animal's natural gaits. His teachings stressed the rider's correct position and balance as crucial for effective communication with the horse.

François Robichon de La Guérinière's work represents a significant milestone in the development of classical dressage, and his principles continue to influence equestrian training to this day.

Unfortunately the Tuileries Palace, which housed the riding academy, was destroyed by fire during the Paris Commune in 1871. In 1883, the ruins of the palace were completely razed.

Today, the site where the Tuileries Palace and its Manège once stood is part of the open area between the Louvre Museum and the Jardin des Tuileries. Visitors can still enjoy the beautiful Jardin des Tuileries, which remains a popular attraction in Paris.

The OLD MASTERS

BY ELAINE HENEY

www.elaineheneybooks.com

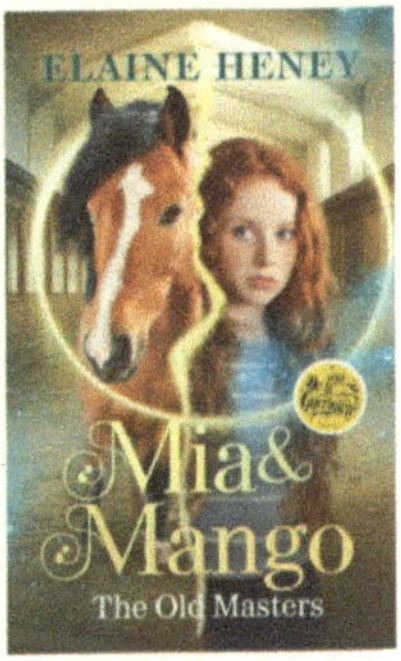

THE 6 CONNEMARA ADVENTURES

by award-winning author, Elaine Heney

www.elaineheneybooks.com

ND - #0440 - 091225 - C4 - 198/129/10 - PB - 9781917234610 - Gloss Lamination